THE POETIC MUSEUM
Reviving Historic Collections

THE POETIC MUSEUM

Reviving Historic Collections

Julian Spalding

Prestel
Munich · London · New York

Front jacket: Joseph Cornell, *Soap Bubble Set*, 1936 mixed media, h. 15 $^3/_4$ × w. 14 $^1/_4$ in.
© The Wadsworth Atheneum Museum of Art, Hartford, CT. Gift of Henry and Walter Keney.

Prestel-Verlag
Mandlstrasse 26
D-80802 Munich
Germany
Tel.: (89) 38-17-09-0
Fax.: (89) 38-17-09-35
www.prestel.de

4 Bloomsbury Place
London
WC1A 2QA
Tel.: (020) 7323 5004
Fax.: (020) 7636 8004

175 Fifth Avenue, Suite 402
New York
NY 10010
Tel.: (212) 995 2720
Fax.: (212) 995 2733
www.prestel.com

Library of Congress Control Number: 2001096182

Prestel books are available worldwide. Please contact your nearest bookseller or any of the above
addresses for information concerning your local distributor.

Editorial direction: Philippa Hurd
Editing: Mary Scott

Design and typesetting: EDV-Fotosatz Huber/Verlagsservice G. Pfeifer, Germering
Printing and binding: Druckerei Huber, Dießen

Printed in Germany

ISBN: 3-7913-2678-3

Contents

Acknowledgments

Among the many people who have helped me with this book, both intentionally and inadvertently, I would like to thank in particular Louise Greenberg, my literary agent, who tirelessly criticised and supported this book to ensure that it could and would reach a wider readership; Maurice Davies and David Phillips who both gave me crucial professional encouragement at an early stage in the manuscript; Philippa Hurd, who saw that I had depicted a mountain range, not one mountain; and Mary Scott, who cleared away all the wisps of mist on its slopes; and, lastly, my wife, Gillian, without whose love this book would not have been written at all.

Introduction

Readers may wonder why anyone would want to write a book about museums, let alone read one. Those who are interested in pictures or insects or engines might want to read a book about them, but not one about the organisations that keep them. But museums are not just passive receptacles; they are institutions with a long and complex history, imbued with all sorts of peculiar, ingrown practices, many of which date back hundreds of years. Most importantly, museums select what they collect and therefore influence what we think about the past. Had the first curators of the British Museum, for example, valued Persian carpets more than the Parthenon Frieze, the development of British culture might have been different. John Ruskin's promotion of Byzantine Gothic could have been central, not eccentric, and modern English buildings might then have been richly decorated, not plain and embellished only with a free-standing, monumental Henry Moore. After all, the great pattern traditions of Islam are close, in many ways, to both Celtic and Gothic art, which many consider more native to England than the figurative art of Greece and Rome. Had it not been for the Victoria & Albert Museum, which showed Islamic alongside medieval art, we might never have had the wallpaper designs of William Morris, who was greatly inspired by the collections of that museum. Museums are not fixtures but creations; they influence, often subliminally, our whole view of culture.

The common view is that, once established, museums cannot be changed, which is another reason for not reading a book about them. But museums are changing all the time. When it opened 250 years ago, the British Museum was first and foremost a library illustrated with collections that included as many stuffed animals as marble statues. The creations of nature, then generally held to be the work of God, were considered just as important as the productions of humanity, so much so that enthusiasts eventually persuaded the government to build a magnificent new museum in South Kensington devoted to this branch of knowledge – the British Museum of Natural History, now the Natural History Museum. The British Museum did not lose its library function until over a century later. Now its remaining task is to illuminate world cultures through artefacts, a depleted product of the Enlightenment. And, over the last century, the Natural History Museum has changed, too. It used to be packed with hundreds of thousands of specimens arranged in rows in glass cases, but if one visits it today it is teeming with children, and there is hardly a specimen in sight.

The Natural History Museum has maintained its research role, collecting and identifying specimens from around the world, but a visitor to its galleries would never know it. It has, in effect, become two institutions, a research academy behind the scenes and a popular theme park out front. This book is an attempt to reverse this general trend in museums. If this is not done, it will not be long before the Egyptian sculptures in the British Museum are replaced with interactive displays and reproductions. The Smithsonian Institution in Washington has announced that 'Old Glory', the original Star-Spangled Banner, is too fragile to be suspended and will have to be removed from view until they can find a way of showing it safely. Why can they not work out how to do this before they take it down, or devise a way to show it while it is being conserved? After all it is *the* icon of America. If we can send a probe to Saturn and operate on an eye, we can certainly find a way of displaying an old flag so that people can see it while ensuring it survives for posterity. But there is, at present, no guarantee that this wonderful relic will be put back on show. Why was there no public outcry about this? Have we ceased to value artefacts from the past? If so, we could be witnessing the end of museums as we have known them. If this happens, museums will have themselves to blame, for not making sure their collections are still treasured in the hearts and minds of the people.

There is no law that says museums have to continue to exist. Many of the museums we know best today were founded before the invention of photography, sound recording, colour printing and film, let alone computers, virtual reality and jet aircraft, yet many curators still act and collect as if these inventions had never been made. They do so partly because their ideas are rooted in the Enlightenment, when the world about us was still full of uncharted territories. But a stuffed kangaroo or a Japanese print or a dinosaur bone will no longer automatically draw crowds filled with amazement. Nor, perhaps, would those visitors who thronged museums a couple of hundred years ago have attended in such numbers had they been able to hop on a plane to see a kangaroo for themselves, or buy a book of colour reproductions of Japanese prints, or watch, in the comfort of their own homes, a computer simulation of a predatory dinosaur sinking its teeth into its latest victim. Today, museums have to survive among all these competing attractions, when no corner of the world remains unexplored and there is widespread acceptance of the concept of extinction.

Modern technology and its current use in contemporary entertainments might, at first sight, look as though it will supersede most of the recording and communicating functions of museums but, in fact, it opens up exciting new possibilities for both collecting and interpretation. Had digital cameras existed, people in earlier times would surely have used them to record the first night of *King Lear* or the last day of the dodo. Museums can now document in vivid ways the formative events in our own times. They have, however, been remarkably slow to take up this challenge. If they have gone on collecting, they have tended to add to what they already have rather than branch out in new directions. Art museums around the world are full of paintings, drawings, prints and sculptures because that is what they have always collected, but remarkably few have photographs, let alone modern graphics or computer art. When museums do venture into new fields, their efforts often seem idiosyncratic. It is not immediately obvious to an outsider why the British Museum, the resting home for great sculptures of antiquity, is acquiring examples of credit cards. Faced with the plethora of modern production, many museums have simply thrown in the towel. Collections are being frozen or, worse, abandoned. Museums either resign themselves to becoming period pieces and put as much of their collections as they can out in displays that emulate their appearance a century earlier, or they turn themselves into high-tech, interactive theme parks and put most of their collections into storage.

This book makes the case that collections are at the heart of museums, not just because they contain wonderful things that can be a joy to look at and learn from, but also because we need museums to go on collecting. There can be no substitute for the experience of seeing with your own eyes the paintings of Leonardo da Vinci, the beaks of the finches that gave Darwin his first inkling of the theory of evolution, or the worn shoes that victims of the Holocaust took off before they entered the gas chamber. Once seen and felt and, as far as one is able, comprehended, such sights can be unforgettable. Creating such flowers of feeling and understanding in the minds of each visitor is the challenge facing museums in the 21st century. I envisage, in this book, a new age of museums. I have called them 'poetic' because they will not be categorical or didactic, but will draw out the profounder, more elusive meanings inherent in so many artefacts from our past. There are countless different ways in which this can be done, but museums have barely begun to realise their potential as storytellers and communicators. They contain many of the most remarkable things in the world, yet many visitors traipse through them as if they were in a railway station, barely engaging with what is around them. People leave Disneyland knowing exactly what has been on offer, with smiles on their faces, talking about their favourite experiences. What expressions does one see on the faces of visitors as they leave the world's great museums? More often than not a look of weariness mixed with relief, and a roving eye searching for somewhere to sit down, and have a nice cup of tea.

This book is written for the users of museums, both those who want an enjoyable and rewarding visit, and those who want to research subjects in depth. My aim is to explore why museums are the way they are, and how they could be changed so that they could serve all their users much better. I want society itself to become more ambitious for its museums, because 30 years of working in them has taught me how often they fail to tell the world about the wonders they contain. Brought up on a public-housing estate on the southern outskirts of London, museums offered me wider horizons. I would save up my pocket money for the train fare to central London to visit the great museums, which were then all free. I might not have gone at all, and certainly not as often, had there been a charge to go in. My background has taught me to be particularly sensitive to the advantages that education, class, wealth, race and where you live can bring, as far as access to culture is concerned. This is not just a question of packaging. People will go to museums if they are interested in what they contain. Not long into my career, I realised that the contents of museums would have to be changed if they wanted to reach a wider public. But this does not mean that museums have to limit themselves to areas of culture already categorised as popular, and put on a diet of dinosaur shows interleaved with Royal wedding dresses. It proved perfectly possible, for example, to triple attendances at Manchester City Art Gallery by expanding, not contracting, its intellectual and aesthetic ambitions, despite the building's tomb-like presence, with its blank windows and relentless, brooding classicism.

I also discovered, early in my career, the writings of John Ruskin, the Victorian art critic and social commentator, who anticipated many positive aspects of the modern museum, such as handling and travelling collections. He designed little carts for these so that they could be easily wheeled about. He created a little gem of a museum for the cutlers of Sheffield, which contained mineral specimens and old master paintings, bird engravings and illuminated missals, photographs and plaster casts, to demonstrate that Darwin was wrong in believing that creation was a product of self-interest. Ruskin believed that creation was the manifestation of a divine moral order. For him, museums were essentially educational institutions for the general public, but more about ideas and feelings than categories of learning. So the seeds of the poetic museum were sown in my mind. The subsequent successes, as I groped towards realising my ideas, were almost as frustrating as the failures, because I never seemed to achieve the sustained development I dreamed of, with everyone in the museum learning through a process of creative discovery. Partly this was due to cutbacks in public funding, but the failure of museums to shield themselves from some of the worst of these was, to some extent, an indication of their failure to prove their worth. Museums have difficulty making their case because they lack a unifying purpose. They are riven with internal disputes, as anyone who has worked in them or with them knows, like a spider with a brain in each leg, straddled by impotent directors and a prey to opinionated boards.

I well remember, when I was first interviewed for the post of Director of the Victoria & Albert Museum in London, being greeted by the Chairman of the Board, Lord Carrington, who was also running Nato at the time, with the introductory comment, 'We don't want any ideas, you know. We've got the ideas. We want someone to carry them out.' The successful candidate, Elizabeth Esteve Coll, who came from a library rather than a museum background, proceeded to do what the Board wanted and sacked all the Museum's senior curatorial staff. It was seen by many as a watershed in the profession: the end of traditional curatorship. It was true that the V&A did have management problems, but getting rid of its leading curatorial expertise was not the answer. What the V&A needed was professional direction, not professional cleansing. Now the role of the museum director itself is under threat. Some boards have decided not to appoint one at all: the Los Angeles County Museum of Art, one of the biggest in the United States, now has a non-professional as its chief executive; and Glasgow, after years of radical development, on the whim of a new political leadership, decided in 1998 to abolish entirely the post of museum director, which I held at the time, along with the directorships of Libraries, Theatres, Parks and Recreation, and replaced us all with a leisure management-style system. This book is written partly to make the case that museums do need directors, quite simply because they have a direction to take. What I have attempted to articulate here is a philosophical basis for that new direction.

Julian Spalding
Edinburgh, January 2002

A 'Devil's Toenail', or a fossil of the extinct oyster, *Gryphaea Arcuata*.
National Museums of Scotland

CHAPTER ONE

Old Things and Old Thoughts

Museums are not just packed with things from the past; they are riddled with past thoughts. Everything in them has a reason for being there and not necessarily one that would interest us, or even occur to us today. It is tempting to think that museums do not change because their collections stay the same. In fact, they are changing invisibly all the time because, though the specimens might be pinned down, our thoughts about them cannot be. The original collectors of ladies' fashions, prehistoric burials or microscopic moths would surely have been surprised to learn that people in the future would be studying them avidly for evidence of sexual oppression, their DNA structure and declining biological diversity. Visitors today are increasingly beginning to wonder why they should look at rows of glasses or guns, fossils or fire engines, and many simply do not bother. Some museums, in response, are putting their collections into storage and replacing them with theatrical and interactive displays in an attempt to keep their public. This is almost invariably a waste, because it is always possible to inspire interest in even the most commonplace object by looking at it from a fresh perspective. Mystery is at one's elbow, and wells deep within museums. The challenge for museums today is to find ways to revive interest in their historic collections. But they can only begin to do this if they find out why their collections are there in the first place.

The visitors who first entered the British Museum's doors had a very different world picture in their minds than those who walk around it today. The museum was founded in 1753, two centuries after Copernicus had proposed that the earth went around the sun, but a hundred years before Charles Darwin realised we shared an ancestry with apes. Though enquiring minds from Leonardo da Vinci onwards considered fossils to be petrified living matter, they had no idea how old they were. They thought that the shells and plants found buried in rocks had been turned to stone sometime during the process of creation or, most probably, at the time of the Flood, for which they gave current proof, for fossils of sea creatures could be found on mountain tops. Less enquiring minds thought that fossils were evidence of Satan's work, just as it was widely believed that jewels were chips off the walls of the heavenly city of God. It was not until the fourth year of the French Republic, in September 1796, that Georges Cuvier demonstrated to his fellow scientists in Paris that there had been other revolutions in the past, and that some fossils were of creatures that had become extinct, thereby undermining, at a stroke, the concept of the perfection of God's creation. Forty years earlier, visitors to the British Museum had no inkling of this. They would have dismissed as incredible the idea that the fossil illustrated at the beginning of this chapter was the petrified remains of an extinct oyster, just as readily and confidently as we dismiss their popularly held belief that it was a devil's toenail. The things in museums might not change, but our ideas about them can, and often do.

The British Museum's rapidly accumulating collections were a by-product of the birth of modern science, when exploration led to revelations in whatever direction it took. Ephraim Chambers, an apprentice globe-maker from Kendal, compiled the first modern encyclopaedia in 1728. Diderot transformed this into his great *Encyclopédie,* which appeared in France, in 35 volumes, from 1751 to 1776. Diderot thought religion was the enemy of knowledge. No wonder the Church and the State were alarmed. One of his books, *Pensées Philosophiques,* was burned at the order of the Parliament of Paris in 1746, and in 1749 he was imprisoned for three months. Undaunted, he continued his studies, arguing that we do not have to accept our lot but can improve it. He proposed, for example, that blind people could learn to read through their sense of touch, a century before Louis Braille developed the means for them to do so. Knowledge, he believed, could conquer the world. Museums, as a vehicle for popular education, were to become a priority of the French Revolution.

The Early Years of the Louvre

The Louvre was for centuries the major palace of the French Royal Family, based upon a much altered and extended fortress built in 1200. Though the picture collection had been open to the public for decades, the whole building was appropriated during the Revolution and the major public spaces turned into a museum. The transformation was remarkably rapid. On 10 August 1792, the Bourbon monarchy collapsed. Nine days later, the decree to create the National Museum of France was declared. In October, the Minister of the Interior, Jean-Marie Rolard, wrote to the painter Jacques-Louis David defining the aims of the new museum: 'This museum must demonstrate the nation's great riches ... France must extend its glory through the ages and to all peoples. The National Museum will embrace knowledge in all its manifold beauty and will be the admiration of the Universe. By embodying these good ideas, worthy of a free people ... the museum ... will become among the most powerful illustrations of the French Republic.'

Napoleon Bonaparte made it one of his objectives to realise this ambition. His military campaign in Egypt was well equipped with scholars, archaeologists and artists. It was Napoleon's soldiers who discovered the Rosetta stone and, realising its significance, sent it to Cairo, where it was seized by the British along with other Egyptian treasures. It now resides in the British Museum and not the Louvre, for which it was destined. (Many of the treasures in museums are essentially loot. Lord Gowrie, when Minister of Arts, rejected the Greek government's request for the return of the Elgin Marbles, with the remark, 'I know it's loot, but it's our loot'.) Napoleon marched through Italy seizing all the treasures he could in his aim to make the Louvre the greatest museum the world has ever seen. In 1798 the *Laocoön*, the *Horses of St Mark's* and the *Apollo Belvedere* were exhibited in the Louvre under a banner which read, 'Monuments of Ancient Sculpture. Greece gave them up. Rome lost them. Their fate has changed twice. It will not change again.' After Napoleon's fall Italy clamoured for their restitution. The famous sculptor, Antonio Canova, personally headed the mission sent by Pope Pius VII in 1815 to bring the treasures back, in which he was largely successful. Many had been ripped from churches, but the Pope did not return them all to their original locations. He appropriated Raphael's *Transfiguration* and Caravaggio's *Deposition*, for example, for his own Vatican museums, where the *Laocoön* also now resides. The Louvre demonstrates vividly in its early years the double-headed motivation behind many museums at that time as a vehicle for both popular education and personal and political ambition.

Museums proliferated in the 19th century to enable a wide public to see the latest, exciting discoveries, as the natural and cultural history of the world came into focus. The perfect expressions of this are the two great pairs of almost identical museums that flank the Maria-Theresian-Platz in the centre of Vienna: one, the Kunsthistorisches Museum, charts the history of Empire; the other, the Natural History Museum, contains virtually every species of animal, stuffed or bottled, known to man in displays that have not changed since it was founded in 1889. In 1846, James Smithson, a modest Englishman, gave the then celestial sum of half-a-million dollars to the American Government to found a museum for 'the increase and diffusion of knowledge among men'. So the Smithsonian Institution in Washington was

15

founded, later to become the most comprehensive museum service in the world. The British Museum was, by then, a century old, and already suffering space problems. In 1860, Richard Owen, the Superintendent of the natural history collections at the museum, complained to a Parliamentary Committee that 'the whole intellectual world this year has been excited by a book on the origin of species; and what is the consequence? Visitors come to the British Museum, and they say, "Let us see all these varieties of pigeons: where is the tumbler, where is the pouter?", and I am obliged with shame to say, "I can show you none of them."… As to showing you the varieties of those species, or any of those phenomena that would aid one at getting at that mysteries of mysteries, the origin of species, our space does not permit.' More recently, the queues that formed to see specimens of moon rock brought back after the first landing, when they were toured on exhibition around Britain, give one some idea of what public interest must have been like in the 19th century, as discovery after discovery was put out on display. In the Age of Enlightenment, new animals were continually being discovered, along with new peoples and cultures, vistas undreamt of were opening up at the end of microscopes and telescopes, and the past was a daring new book whose pages people had only just begun to turn. The world was full of wonder, and museums were its portal.

New museums were opening all the time. Richard Owen achieved his wish before he died. In 1878, all the specimens belonging to the departments of botany, zoology, palaeontology and mineralogy were transferred to South Kensington to create the new British Museum of Natural History. Unencumbered by stuffed animals and pressed flowers, the British Museum could become, as its greatest director, Sir Antonio Panizzi, had envisaged, 'an institution for the diffusion of culture', and culture alone. This, above all, for Panizzi, meant books, as he was first and foremost a great librarian. He created the famous Reading Room during the time he was a director there from 1856 to 1866 although, sadly, he failed to persuade the government to provide the money to make it a lending library, too. As a young man, he had escaped from Italy to Britain to avoid imprisonment for allegedly killing a chief constable in a revolutionary fracas – his career, if nothing else, a tribute to the entrepreneurial spirit of those times. Once a revolutionary always a revolutionary, and Panizzi remained a dedicated egalitarian until the end. His aim was to ensure that anyone, however poor, could 'have the same means of indulging his learned curiosity, of consulting the same authorities, of fathoming the most intimate enquiry as the richest man in the country'.

Culture was now becoming as interesting a field for exploration as nature. After Darwin, many saw evolution at work in the progress of civilisation.

Museums had previously collected 'primitive' cultural artefacts as curios, and as illustrations of the errors of the heathen. Now these items were avidly collected to show the progress of mankind. The Pitt Rivers Museum in Oxford is a perfect example of this approach, preserved virtually intact from Victorian times. In the decade after the publication of the *Origin of Species* in 1859, General Pitt Rivers collected everything he could that showed what he called 'the living scroll of human progress'. So one case in the museum details the history of fire-making, another the evolution of the firearm. He invented the word 'typology' to describe the sequence of gradual improvements that he hoped to discover in everything man had made and done. New ideas like this even began to influence the bastion of learning at the British Museum, now a century old.

Before Darwin, the British Museum had no doubts about the order of human culture. There was the Department of Greek and Roman Antiquities, and all other cultures were lumped together as 'Oriental'. This included not just Chinese and Indian artefacts, as one would expect, but also all the Ancient Egyptian, Assyrian, ethnographic, North and South American material as well as, more surprisingly, the European medieval Christian collections, and finally, thrown in for good measure, anything British. Up until the mid-19th century, Britain was regarded as barbarous and simply not worthy of study. But the idea that culture could have evolved began to take hold during the 19th century, and a new hierarchy emerged. Greece and Rome were still on top but, in 1866, the first British Department was formed, although it still encompassed European medieval antiquities and all ethnography. Britain might by then have been the largest Empire the world had ever seen, but culturally speaking, in comparison with the Greeks, it had, according to the intellectuals who ran the British Museum, achieved little more than medieval monks or the tribes of the Amazon or Borneo.

The concept of a hierarchy of human culture seems strange to us today. Few, for example, would consider the Lindisfarne Gospels 'inferior' to a Roman mosaic. The idea that a 'savage' could be 'noble' was not new in the 19th century, but we would not now use the term 'savage' at all. Nor would we automatically assume that a society with no technical aids was necessarily less 'advanced' than ourselves, and we would certainly hesitate to call it 'primitive'. We are no longer nearly so sanguine about the possibility of human progress, nor even of the benefit of scientific discoveries. Nuclear physics and genetic engineering have taught us that these can expose dangers as well as save us from them. And the genocides of the 20th century have made us painfully aware of the limitations of the civilising process. We no longer regard ourselves as central to creation, but as minute particles on an isolated planet. Over and above all that, we have ceased, in the last half-century, to have a confident and easy relationship with our natural surroundings. For the first time in human history, we have come to regard ourselves as a disease on the surface of the planet. Many even question the value of scientific study, the very basis on which all our major museums were founded. The battle that led to Galileo's enforced recantation of his 'suspicion' that the earth went round the sun, still rages. In 1987, the Supreme Court of America overturned a Louisiana Statute by ruling that creation science, which that state wanted to be taught in its schools, was a religious belief and therefore could not be taught as a science. The Roman Catholic Church did not revoke their condemnation of Galileo until 1992. A recent survey showed that 47 per cent of all Americans, and a quarter of college graduates, believe that we did not evolve but were created by God a few thousand years ago. Museums still have an important role to play in spreading enlightenment, but they cannot do so blindly, in the name of scientific progress, sweeping aside all other interpretations of experience as manifestations of ignorance. What is needed, today, is the post-Enlightenment museum – one that can be equally revealing to the poet and the scientist.

Since museums are about increasing understanding, any consideration of their future has to ask the fundamental question: is understanding important to us today? If so, the understanding of what? Knowledge, as we have seen, has a short history. Mankind has existed as a species for possibly 200,000 years, no one knows for sure. Up until as recently as 30,000 years ago, we lived alongside another species of mankind. But we only discovered that we did a mere 150 years ago, when the bones of Neanderthal man were found. The idea that every living creature has a common ancestry and is continually evolving, including ourselves today, came as much of a shock to us as did the notion that the earth was not static but turning. It is now a truism to say that nothing is permanent, but museums still fondly cling to the belief that they are fixtures, bastions even, against change. The British Museum is no exception; it reiterates the mantra of its founders, claiming that 'its collections are held together and in perpetuity in their entirety'. Yet in 1878, they lost all their natural history specimens and, in 1997, all their books. Both of these sections were originally thought to be central to the museum's purpose, and constituted by far the largest part of its holdings, numerically at least. Now they are regarded as irrelevant to its main function. Since its foundation, it is true that the British Museum has gone on getting bigger, but only physically. As far as its intellectual ambitions are concerned, it has shrunk considerably. It began as a repository of all knowledge, and believed in the unity of knowledge. Visitors in the 18th century would have seen more stuffed giraffes than Egyptian mummies, and they would have been able to read virtually any book in the world. Today, the British Museum 'diffuses culture' through artefacts alone.

The British Museum was originally modelled on a concept of a museum that dates back to antiquity. The first museum we know of existed in Alexandria in the 3rd century BCE. It appears to have been part of an attempt, under the auspices of Ptolomy I Soter, to bring all fields of human knowledge together in one place. The library was its most famous feature. The Greek historian, Strabo, left an account of its complex of buildings, banqueting halls, gardens and covered walkways. As a whole, it sounds more like a monastery or university than a museum. It had a priest at its head and was not a public institution in any way that we would understand the term. The idea that one institution can encompass all knowledge is now not just impractical but redundant. Collections do not have to be all in one place for people to access them. It does not matter where they are or even who administers them, as they are becoming increasingly accessible through the computer. How Diderot would have loved the computer – all those facts, all those cross references, all those interconnections at the tips of one's fingers! Compass, the British Museum's new interactive database, will enable the public to explore its collections in both conventional and interdisciplinary, thematic ways. But you do not need to go to the British Museum to see it; Compass is on the web. You only need to go to the British Museum if you want to see the real things for yourself, and millions do. The British Museum attracts 6 million visits a year. By 2007, it calculates that there will be 7 million. By 2020, there could be as many as 10 million. Sir Antonio Panizzi once remarked that a museum is not a show. But the British Museum is left being just that, now that the library has gone and people can access information about its collections through the web. Why should anyone visit it but to see what is on show? And all it has left to show is its collection of cultural artefacts – the British Museum's unique asset and the sole carrier of its message.

These artefacts used to provide only part of the picture: they were illustrations in a wider search for understanding. The collection of the Danish physician and antiquarian, Ole Worm, which was absorbed into the Royal Kunstkammer in Copenhagen in 1655 and later formed the basis for the National Museum of Denmark, contained fabulous objects such as an agate that happened to look like an image of Christ on the Cross flanked by Mary and St John. But Ole Worm was interested in the truth as well as wonder. He used his collection to prove to the world that straight horns did not come from unicorns, as had been popularly believed, but from a species of arctic whale, much to the chagrin of many Scandinavian fishermen who had profiteered for years by supplying evidence of the fabled beast.

The natural tendency of museums, if they do not know something, is to hide the fact, in the hope that some time in the future they will be able to declare it. Admissions of ignorance, they fear, will only sully their status as temples of knowledge. An exhibition of Dead Sea Scrolls in Glasgow in 1998 included the only fragment that refers to a 'pierced Messiah', which some scholars believe could be a near-contemporary written reference to the historical Jesus. But the curators from the Israeli Museum who had lent the material insisted that, since its relationship with Jesus had not been proven, only passing reference could be made to this theory, buried at the end of an accurate but boring label. Facts had to come first. So most visitors went round that exhibition unaware of the possible significance of this tiny, brown scrap of parchment, their minds unstirred by the wonder of what we do not know about the past. Museums in the future will need to promote doubt with delight. There are good scientific reasons why they should do so, because there is still a surprising amount that we do not know about the past.

The Parthenon Frieze in the British Museum

Visitors to the British Museum today are informed, as an undisputed fact, that the Parthenon frieze represents one of the great ceremonial processions of Ancient Athens. Every four years, the gigantic gold and ivory statue of the goddess, which stood in the inner sanctum of the Parthenon, was dressed in a new robe. The frieze shows a folded cloth being handed over to a man. So everything seems to fit. But it does not. Contemporary accounts indicate that cavalry did not take part in this procession, but there are 192 horsemen on the Parthenon frieze, which has led some scholars to assert that it celebrates the famous Battle of Marathon, when thousands of Persians were slain, but only 192 Greeks died. And there are other interpretations of the frieze as well. Could it show King Erecheus, who sacrificed one of his daughters to ensure an Athenian victory over Thrace? If so, the robe being presented is not Athena's, but the garment in which the young girl will be led to the altar. The British Museum favours the most mundane interpretation (even though it is unusual for sculptures on sacred buildings to represent contemporary events), but they are wrong to present this as the only interpretation. The truth is that we do not know what this world-famous sculptural frieze represents, or even what it looked like original-ly when it was brightly painted. It is in a museum's interest to emphasise what it does not know, because one looks at something all the harder if one does not know what it is. Objects can be especially intriguing if no one knows what they are, and one is invited to participate in interpret-ing the evidence.

Our origins are still extremely obscure, and only tantalising fragments re-main of the earliest cultures. Confident in our scientific age, we tend to dis-miss cultures that were built on uncertainties about the world around them, even though these contained much that was profoundly poetic and intensely human. Museums are full of wonderful things, from the pediment sculptures on the Parthenon to the golden jewellery of the Aztecs, which were made by people *because* they did not know the earth went round the sun. No artist today could carve the sun's chariot rising in the east, or mould the gold raft that would carry the sun back to the dawn after it had set, with the same profundity of feeling as sculptors did in Ancient Greece or Mexico, simply because, for us, the dawn no longer brings with it a dai-ly, magnificent mystery. The Australian traditional Aborigines, by far the oldest living culture in the world, still believe that the red glow at sunset is the light cast by the souls of the dead as they leave and return to the under-world. Fifty years ago, Aboriginal skulls were still being exhibited in Euro-pean museums in displays illustrating early stages of human evolution. What do we accept today that our successors will find unbelievable? There will always be something new to find out. The development of computers, in-stead of replacing the brain, has actually revealed how remarkably little we know about it. One reason why museums have to exhibit uncertainties is to enable them to keep pace with discovery. Most museums have what they call 'permanent' displays. These contain their permanent collections and are, nowadays, often installed in such a way as to make them difficult to change. But permanence can be the wrong starting point, even when a museum is apparently 'eternal' in its values.

There are sound educational reasons why museums today need to place greater emphasis on what they do not know, rather than what they do. Cat-egorical presentations demonstrating variations in the appearance of fres-coes in Florence or butterflies in Borneo can be off-putting, especially to visitors who do not know why they are looking at these displays in the first place. Museums would have a better chance of captivating the attention of a wider audience if they used as their starting point the ignorance we have all shared, and must share. Awareness of ignorance is essential if we are to begin to understand the thoughts and feelings of those who lived before our scientific age, and whose productions now provide our museums with their chief attractions. As Diderot apocryphally said on his deathbed, 'the first step towards philosophy is incredulity'. Paradoxically, by abandoning certainty, the post-Enlightenment museum can return to its roots.

Science has stripped most of the wonder from the world we can see around us, which may be one reason why we have become so careless about it. We label things and think we know them, ever since we named the beasts, but the more one looks at a drop of water, or a blade of grass, or gazes into someone else's eyes, the more extraordinary what one is looking at becomes. Darwin once confided to a friend that the sight of a peacock's tail feather made him feel sick. How could such an elaborate and beautiful structure have simply evolved through the luck of the draw of natural selection? The fact that it did need not reduce the wonder we feel when looking at a peacock's tail. On the contrary, it can increase it, especially if it leads us to wider speculations, for example about the impact that the evolution of the eye (the peahen's as well as our own) has had on the appearance of nature as a whole. Museums will continue to have a duty to accumulate knowledge, but their authority will be based more in the future on their openness towards and commitment to learning, not on the weight of their knowledge to date. Anyone with access to a computer can claim that. Far from abandoning their collections, museums can only maintain them by continually reassessing their significance, and by freshly questioning their interpretations of them in the light of the larger role they can play within society as a whole.

The Museum of Tolerance

The Museum of Tolerance in Los Angeles was opened in 1994 as part of the Simon Wiesenthal Centre, a leading human-rights organisation that is particularly active in tracking down Nazis. It is a museum essentially of ideas, not things. Originally, the Centre wanted to create a Holocaust Museum, along the lines of that in Washington, telling the story of what happened to the victims of Nazism, but the State of California, one of its sponsors, demanded that the museum have a wider brief, and deal with contemporary issues of racism and prejudice, particularly in America. To do this the museum found it had to change its displays, and much more rapidly than it had expected.

Upon entering the museum, you are invited to go through either a door marked 'prejudiced' or one marked 'unprejudiced'. If you are cheeky enough to push the one marked 'unprejudiced', you discover it is locked. The guide helpfully reminds you that it is so because we are all prejudiced in one way or another. The introductory display (before a sequence of tableaux leads you inexorably to the door to the gas chamber) explores the origins of prejudice. Much emphasis is given to the power of words, how they can either incite hatred or lead to understanding. So important is vocabulary to this museum that words become, in effect, the artefacts around which the exhibition is built. To make these displays as effective as possible, the museum decided to concentrate on contemporary terms of abuse. It soon discovered, however, after the permanent exhibit had been installed, that abusive slang is changing all the time; a whole new repertoire can be on the streets within six months. Within two years it became clear that substantial alterations had to be made to the displays. To be successful in its mission, this museum has to be capable of change. It has had difficulty keeping up to date.

Museums are living institutions. They have changed a great deal since the Enlightenment. They may never again be at the forefront of knowledge in general, though they can still provide a vital platform where discoveries can be exposed and debated in public. There is still much to be learnt from the treasure-house of the past, but museums can no longer carry out even the lion's share of this research. During the Enlightenment, museums took on an egalitarian educational role. They assumed, quite rightly, the public's interest. This can no longer be taken for granted. But museums still contain what Howard Carter called, when he peered for the first time into Tutankhamun's tomb, 'wonderful things', and they can throw open countless windows onto worlds where the unexplained was the order of the day. By actively doing so, they can help restore the gleam of wonder to our jaded gaze, and reinvigorate our appetite for experiencing life in all its ultimately unfathomable glory. By reviving the open-minded, exploring spirit of their early days, museums can re-enlighten us.

Nereid (back view), from the Nereid Monument, Xanthos, 390–380 BCE,
thought to have escorted the souls of the dead on a wind over the waves to the afterlife
(light areas indicating modern reconstruction).
British Museum

CHAPTER TWO
Grains of Truth

Most visitors today assume that all the collections in museums are genuine, and that everything they tell you about them is true. But, in fact, very few artefacts from the past have come down to us intact. It is not just that most of them have suffered or altered in one way or another, by being damaged, worn or changing colour with age; they have also often been tampered with by people in the past, in an attempt to preserve them or restore them. Only objects made of solid gold have a chance of retaining their original appearance, and almost invariably these are bent or broken, because gold, though incorruptible, has little inner strength. Just a handful of objects in museums are entirely what the label says they are. A 15th-century Italian altarpiece might be exactly that, but it is not the altarpiece that was once the object of veneration. Its original worshippers would surely have been distressed at seeing the Virgin's robe folded in funereal black, when they were used to seeing her wrapped in celestial blues.

A surprising number of museum exhibits are questionable and many, if restored, are blatantly deceptive, but museums are often hesitant to reveal all they know about their collections, especially if this undermines the status of an exhibit. So most museum labels inform the visitor about dates, measurements, materials, and the provenance of the object on display, but hardly any tell how the object has changed since it was first made, and even fewer explain what it meant then and what it could mean today. The challenge museums now face is to see themselves no longer as sole purveyors of the truth, but as seekers after truth on a journey they share with their visitors. When they do this, their whole scope of operation broadens and they can become genuinely inclusive once again. Instead of encouraging their visitors to believe everything they see, it would be better if museums hung over their doors banners reading 'Doubt all you who enter here'.

Few visitors are aware that almost everything visible in most vintage car displays is the comparatively recent, loving product of the technician's workshop. Any rusty parts or worn upholstery have been replaced with new materials. There might be an original chassis underneath but, to all intents and purposes, the visitor could just as well be looking at a reproduction. One of the stars of the Museum of Transport in Glasgow is a sparkling gypsy caravan, but nothing the visitor can see is original, and even its chamfered glass windows have been immaculately recreated. Simply placing another gypsy caravan, unrestored, a sorry exhibit with broken windows, weatherbeaten woodwork and tattered, faded upholstery, on display beside the restored one, would make the point about how museums fictionalise history, but the staff concerned were never happy with this proposal. Museums, like most institutions, take a pride in their appearance, even if it is false. It is not necessarily wrong to restore something to its original appearance; it is just that visitors have a right to know what they are looking at. Motor-car enthusiasts not only keep their vehicles in mint condition, but drive them to rallies, where they can be seen by more people; and on the road, not in aspic in a museum. A locomotive roaring along a track at full steam beats the experience of seeing one stationary in a museum any day, whether it is beautifully restored or a sad old wreck.

Collectors often refer to items that have survived virtually intact as being 'museum-quality specimens'. Stamps and coins are valued more highly if they are approaching mint condition, partly because this is an easy way to measure rarity. Yet things that show their age are often much more evocative. Many museums have ancient Egyptian bead necklaces, still in pristine condition, glowing with all their brilliant mineral colours. The Metropolitan Museum of Art in New York, however, has one of the much rarer collars made of real leaves and flowers, of which the bead necklaces were imitations. Scientists have identified olives, cornflowers and poppies among the pale brown leaves and petals. Looking at it, you sense the presence of the hand that picked them and arranged them, despite their faded appearance. Their original colours, in one's imagination, glow more brightly around the neck of the girl who wore them, than the bead necklace, still shining gaudily, can ever do.

Lübeck Cathedral suffered a direct hit during an allied bombing raid in the Second World War, when its bells crashed to the ground. In the grim aftermath, the uppermost motive in most people's minds must have been to sweep away all the debris and rebuild the Cathedral as it had been before. But the sight of the bells stopped them in their tracks. The fall had bent and broken them as if they had been made of marzipan. They were at once a phenomenal and poetic sight, a symbol of all that had happened at that time. So the people of Lübeck left their old bells where they had fallen, and rebuilt the cathedral around their story. The Cathedral now looks as if the war had never happened, but everyone hurries to see the stricken bells.

The cathedrals of Europe have been almost entirely rebuilt over the centuries. Masons have been continually replacing their stonework, so that a surprising amount of what we can see in them today is only a version of the original, sometimes as many as four or more times removed. I saw an extreme case of this when visiting Kumamoto Castle in southern Japan. I noticed concrete sections in the foundations. The whole castle had burnt down in the 19th century and been totally reconstructed in the 20th. But my host insisted that it was 17th century. The fact that it was a modern version did not, for her, diminish the castle's authenticity. The concept of authenticity in the West is a product of our materialist philosophy. The Shinto shrine at Ise in Japan has been rebuilt every 20 years since the late 17th century, symbolising the regeneration of its spirit. The value of museums is rather diminished if one believes that one can preserve the past simply by copying it.

Copying has become a pejorative term in the West, but it was not always so. John Ruskin employed 'copyists' without disparaging them, for the museum he created in Sheffield, to paint versions of the frescoes he so admired in Italy, since he could not transport them. The aim of these was not to produce slavish reproductions, but to express the feelings the originals inspired. The museum, therefore, contains not painted copies of whole frescoes, but intense little watercolours of details that Ruskin was particularly moved by, such as an angel's wing or a wild flower growing beside the Virgin's gown. They are interpretations, not imitations. We call the conductor's or the director's version of a performance an 'interpretation', but if an artist tried to imitate the *Mona Lisa*, not as a forgery but as an interpretation of what he or she thought Leonardo was trying to express, there would be no place for such efforts in our canon of values. The same purist approach would appear very strange in music: if, for example, an original recording existed of Beethoven's Ninth Symphony and that was the only one that could ever be played. It is not purity that museums require, but clarity. Museums *are* interpreters of the past and they need to develop this aspect of their work positively and creatively.

To bring the past back to life, museums cannot just rely on setting out the fragments of it that remain. The key question about a restoration or a reconstruction is whether it diminishes or enhances our appreciation of the original. The challenge to a museum is to make what is evoked as authentic as it can be. The Natural History Museum in Basel has commissioned some convincing but imaginary taxidermy of prehistoric beasts. The chalicotherium, a vast, 15-foot high creature, a cross between a horse and a sloth, looks like nothing you have ever seen on earth. It is extremely convincing, however, because the fur, ears, nostrils and eyes, and the position of the bones and muscles under the skin, are so well detailed. Looking at this creature, you feel you are breathing the air of another age. It is difficult to get this impression when staring at a skeleton, that has been rebuilt from fragments of fossil bone. Authentic reconstructions based on modern analytical techniques offer many exciting possibilities for museums in future. Then visitors will smile when they see an old model of a dinosaur with nicely brushed teeth.

The Manchester Museum

Using forensic techniques, John Prag and Richard Neave, working at the Manchester Museum, have been able to recreate faces from ancient skulls, famously the head of Philip of Macedonia, but it is difficult to judge the accuracy of most of their efforts because no detailed contemporary visual records exist for comparison. There is one exception, however. Egyptian mummies during the Roman period were faced with portraits, not masks, many of which look as though they were painted from life. Prag and Neave have reconstructed several of the faces from the skulls within these mummies, and exhibited them alongside the portraits painted of them when they were alive. The similarities are unnerving and very moving. Looking from one to the other is like turning from the person being painted to the portrait on the easel. It is as though you were looking over the artist's shoulder and could watch him capturing a likeness faithfully here, or idealising it slightly there. When you look at the portrait you see it through the eyes of another human being, albeit someone who lived many centuries ago. This additional living presence stays with you, so that when you turn to look again at the reconstructed head, it appears to breathe.

Most old paintings in galleries, like cars in transport museums and cathedrals in cities, have been restored several times during their existence. Until comparatively recently, restorations were carried out by painters. Professional restorers did not exist until the 19th century, and conservation only started to become a science in the 1930s. If a painting had been damaged, a painter was considered the best person to repair it because he or she would have the necessary training in what was then seen as a traditional skill. Historical changes in styles and techniques were not so carefully differentiated then, and nothing like so much emphasis was placed on the 'hand of the master'. Paintings were simply another commodity and, though highly valued and invested in, the artist's intentions were treated much less respectfully than they are today.

The Rembrandt Research Project

Successive catalogues raisonnées of Rembrandt's work have, over the last century, attributed at the most 711 and at the least 470 works to this artist. In 1969, the Rembrandt Research Project began trying to distinguish, once and for all, which paintings were by Rembrandt, which were by his workshop, which were by followers and imitators and which were fakes. They have found the task much more difficult than they thought. Thirty years later it is still incomplete. Perhaps the Team's attempts to distinguish between Rembrandt's own work and that of his circle may have been the very thing preventing them from resolving these problems. Authenticity of authorship was not such an issue for artists at that time as it has become for us.

Our view of art has changed. Among the millions of artists working today, we now value those with an original voice. We do not expect these artists to be comforting because our world is not. As a result of the Rembrandt Project, many of the artist's paintings have recently been reattributed as being not the work of the artist, particularly those that appear to our taste to be sweet. The famous painting, *An Old Man In An Armchair*, dated 1652, still hangs with the other Rembrandts in the National Gallery in London, but it is no longer labelled as Rembrandt. This decision was made on account of its sentimental mood and crude technique, although I cannot see anything crude in the way it has been painted. The sitter's right hand, which is singled out for criticism, is summarily sketched, but there is an aesthetic reason for this. Rembrandt is the only artist I know who greatly exaggerated the differences in scale and detail between a hand held near and one seen further back. He uses this device nowhere more tellingly than here, where the feeling of distance so created is entirely in keeping with the faraway look in the old man's face. He sits quietly lost in thought and overshadowed by fear. I do not find this picture 'sentimental' at all, though it is full of sentiment. Perhaps these scholars, by excluding such 'sentimental' works from the canon, are creating a grimmer Rembrandt to match our expectations of artists today.

The Rembrandt Research Project has had difficulty in completing its task because it has been asking the wrong question. Rembrandt was not an artist of genius working in isolation, but an artist of genius running a workshop. In the same way, museums can be led into a trap by defining their borders too tightly, and excluding everything that is not, as presently understood, authentic. The truth can never be entirely contained. The value of *An Old Man In An Armchair* lies in the profundity with which it explores and expresses feelings of old age. Its truth to our experience of life validates its place in the National Gallery, whether it is solely by Rembrandt, by Rembrandt and his team, or by a much later, unknown artist of brilliance working in an unaccountably anachronistic manner, as the Rembrandt Project has proposed.

We place more and more value now on authenticity. The term 'restorer' is becoming increasingly outlawed; we now have 'conservators'. Obviously, the artist's original handiwork cannot be replicated, and many conservators think it wrong even to imitate it. In Italy, this purist approach has been taken to extremes; everything that is not the original is removed, leaving, in some of the most damaged pictures, only a patchwork of painted areas. This process has now been applied to Leonardo's *Last Supper* of *c.*1495–8, in S. Maria delle Grazie in Milan, a painting that began to deteriorate almost as soon as it was finished, and has been patched up by artists wishing to preserve its original effect ever since. Now it is the authentic shadow of a wreck. At least the conservators have not filled in the lost areas with patches of grey, as they used to do, for example on Cimabue's great *Crucifixion*, which was seriously damaged in the Florence flood, and is now almost impossible to make sense of as a whole. The frescoes by Masaccio in the Brancacci Chapel of *c.*1427, have recently been beautifully restored so that, if you go up close, you can see the areas of original paint loss have been filled in, not with the broad brush strokes of the original, but with tiny strokes resembling chopped straws, which have the effect of the original at a distance.

Conservators in Britain tend to adopt a more robust attitude to retouching a painting that has been damaged. They are careful, of course, to ensure that anything that they put on can be easily and safely removed later. They take pains to retouch only those areas where paint has been lost so as not to cover up any of the original. But after that, the British way is to recreate as near as possible the appearance of the original, using the same style of brushwork, colour and tone as the rest of the painting. Many famous and familiar paintings are actually much more damaged than they appear. Titian's *Bacchus and Ariadne*, in the National Gallery in London, suffered extensive damage by being rolled up at some time in its history. Whole areas of original paint had come away where the picture was creased, leaving the sky and central figures greatly disfigured. Now, it looks as fresh as if it were painted yesterday. The sky is a brilliant ultramarine and the figures glow with warm flesh tints. A row broke out about the extent of the cleaning when it was put on display, the result of a simple misunderstanding of the structure of oil paintings and the temporary varnishes used to protect them. The same row breaks out each time a famous picture is cleaned, most recently over the Sistine Chapel ceiling. The colours of the Titian and the Michelangelo seem startlingly bright to anyone who had been familiar with these works before, buried as the colours were beneath layers of discoloured varnish and dirt. The cry was that these paintings had been over-cleaned.

It was claimed that irresponsible restorers had cleaned off the top glazes and varnish layers that the artists had used to dampen down the brilliance of the colours. But I know of no museum restorers today who would not stop cleaning immediately they saw traces of original pigment on their swabs. It is also difficult to understand why an artist, especially one as proficient as Titian or Michelangelo, would use such bright colour and then tone it down. They could easily have created a muted effect in the first place. It is also hard to imagine an artist like Titian saying to his patron that he knew the picture was a bit bright, but when the varnish had yellowed in a few decades or so, it would look better! A Renaissance potentate would want the picture to look its best when he paid for it. Michelangelo's Sistine Chapel Ceiling, moreover, is executed in fresco, a technique that effectively makes the picture part of the wall surface. The painting is not *on* the wall but *in* it. No restorer, today, is going to dig into the wall itself while cleaning it!

The *Mona Lisa*

A controversy has recently broken out as to whether or not the *Mona Lisa* should be cleaned. It is currently covered in a layer of varnish that has aged and yellowed. Underneath, the painting is in remarkably good condition. If the discoloured varnish layer were removed, the visitor would be able to see the wonderful misty blue landscape in the distance, about which Leonardo's contemporaries went into such ecstasies on its completion in 1506, but that can now hardly be seen beneath the dirty yellow surface. Varnish is not part of the original picture. It is added as a layer to protect the paint beneath from grime and slight abrasions. It always yellows with age and has to be removed every 70 years or so. This can easily be done without damaging the paint layers underneath. The *Mona Lisa* will have had many new coats of varnish applied during its existence. The one currently covering the surface of the picture has nothing whatever to do with Leonardo. But still the Louvre refuses to clean it, arguing that the picture is well liked in its current, obscured state. They claim that this is clearly good enough for people today, so there is no reason to clean it, no matter what the artist originally intended. This is a disservice to Leonardo and to people today; it betrays a lack of ambition for the role that art can play in people's lives. Paintings in the Renaissance were not meant to look like old masters but were fresh and brilliant of hue.

Kenneth Clark, one-time Director of the National Gallery of London, and a popular figure through his TV series, *Civilisation*, once had the good fortune to see the *Mona Lisa* out of its frame, in daylight. He wrote, 'in the sunshine something of the warm life which Vasari admired comes back to her'. He was remembering Vasari's description of the painting: 'The eyes had that lustre and watery sheen which is always seen in real life, and around them were those touches of red and the lashes which cannot be represented without the greatest subtlety. The nose, with its beautiful nostrils, rosy and tender, seemed to be alive. The opening of the mouth, united by the red of the lips to the tones of the face, seemed not to be coloured but to be living flesh.' As Kenneth Clark added, 'Who would recognise (by this description) the submarine goddess of the Louvre?' Submarine, because of the layers of yellow varnish that discolour her and the thick, green bullet-proof glass behind which she now appears.

Using scientific analysis and modern conservation skills, a trained restorer could reconstruct the *Mona Lisa* as it would have appeared when it left the easel, with its two flanking pillars (the picture was cut down after it was painted) and in the full glory of its fresh colours, unfaded and undimmed. No one would claim that the finished product would be what Leonardo intended, but it would certainly be a valid exercise in trying to understand his intentions, especially if the Louvre persists, perversely, in not cleaning the picture.

Conservators are only just beginning to reconstruct the true glory of the colours of the past. Attempts are being made to simulate the appearance of old pigments, because they are now both hard to find and very expensive. The conservator Anna Hulbert, for example, has devised a method of mixing glass beads with cobalt blue to emulate azurite, which gives one some impression of the magical effect the genuine pigment must have had when spread across the roofs of cathedrals and churches. Modern paints have a brashness and crudeness that makes them look quite different from the colours of the past; their use in reconstructions today is often justified on the grounds that they recreate the gaudy taste of our 'primitive' ancestors. The probable truth is that our predecessors did not love strong colours only for their brightness, but also for their poetic power. Like all things in creation, colours were sensations of wonder, deeply imbued with symbolic meaning. So the Venerable Bede could write, at the beginning of the 8th century, 'violet which imitates the colour of the sky is aptly compared to the desire for heavenly things. Purple, which is made from the blood of shellfish and has even the appearance of blood, represents the mystery of our Lord's Passion. Scarlet, which is a glowing red shade, expresses the virtue of love.' The evidence suggests that the colours of the past had to convey their poetic meaning. It is startling to come across evidence of the taste of the Vikings, that reputedly violent and uncivilised race, as demonstrated by traces of paint found on the sledges placed in ship burials, now in the Viking Ships Museum in Oslo. These intricately carved wooden sledges, now dark brown, were originally painted black and pale grey. But what is unexpected is that the incised depths were painted light and the surfaces dark. One might have expected the light to be on top and dark below, but then one would not have seen the shadows. Painted as they are, the effect of these sledges moving in sunlight must have been breathtaking. As the shadows in the carved patterns shifted, it would have looked as though the magical beasts depicted among them were writhing and alive, as the sledge glided silently across the snow.

The Glyptothek in Munich has been attempting to reconstruct the original appearance of some of the Greek sculptures in their collection, using the microscopic traces of pigment they have discovered on them. The evidence they have found suggests that the young soldiers on the pediment would have had glowing rosy cheeks, bright red lips and long black eyelashes! The attempts they have made so far to reconstruct the appearance of these statues, based on plaster casts, fail to be convincing, however. This is not because the colours they are using are too strong (they might well not be strong enough); it is because they are too crude. We have lost the ancient techniques used to mix colours and apply them. The glamorous make-up of the young Greek soldier looks wrong not because it is seductive, but because it is put on with little finesse, and the pigments used are synthetic. It is quite likely that there is no one in the world today who can paint as well as a Renaissance master, even though work exists to copy from. How can anyone hope, then, to emulate the famed painters of Ancient Greece whose works have all been lost?

The Temple of Aphaia on Aegina

The pediment statues from the Temple of Aphaia on Aegina, a small island in the Saronic Gulf just south of Athens, were discovered in fragments in 1811 and were restored by the Danish neo-classical sculptor, Bertel Thorvaldsen, in Rome between 1816 and 1818. He worked in marble, filling in the smallest fractures, and adding shields, limbs and faces when these were missing, which they often were, just as he saw fit. He then 'aged' the new marble to match the original. It was a seamless recreation, the most ambitious reconstruction ever attempted of a classical group. It became the centrepiece of the new Museum of Ancient Art, called the Glyptothek, when it was opened in Munich in 1830.

In 1910, new excavations at Aegina revealed the pediment's base, showing that Thorvaldsen had put the figures back in the wrong place; one warrior he famously reconstructed as fallen had originally been standing up! Despite these new discoveries, the assembly remained undisturbed till 1962, when the curators decided to dismantle Thorvaldsen's reconstruction. By then they had a political incentive for doing so. Hitler had used the Königsplatz, where the Glyptothek stood, as the focal point for his rallies, partly because of its association with Greek art which, according to the Nazi's distorted propaganda, celebrated a racial ideal they wished Germany to emulate. In an effort to cleanse these associations, Thorvaldsen's additions were removed, without fuss, in the name of authenticity, and a metal-pinned, fragmentary configuration was reassembled in its place. Perhaps a future age will attempt another reconstruction of the pediment from the Temple of Aphaia, using the analysis of the original pigments that were used by Thorvaldsen to bring these wonderful classical sculptures so vigorously to life, leaving the current reconstruction looking like 1960s' Constructivist sculpture.

It is easy to assume that we find eternal truths in museums, but the best we can hope to discover is the search for them, and this is surely more interesting than landing on just one truth (which may subsequently be overturned). The State Museum of Political History of Russia in St Petersburg occupies the building that contains the flat and balcony from which Lenin conducted the first days of the Russian Revolution. Preserved in its original, simple state, this modest flat was an essential destination for millions of Russian tourists during the Communist era. Now, virtually no one goes there. The curators of the museum have updated the displays with a new ambition 'to form the political culture of society'. They now show the 'truth' as they had to tell it during the Regime, on red panels, side by side with the 'truth' as they now understood it to have happened, on grey panels. In the centre of this new display, installed in 1991, a pile of guns and ammunition is surmounted by an inscription that reads 'God is not in force, but in truth'. Further into this museum, I saw that the curators had been keeping the collections up to date. One showcase included fragments of the damaged walls of the villa where President Mikhail Gorbachev had been imprisoned during the failed coup d'état that followed perestroika, and the video he himself had taken of the event. He had insisted that the museum take this material because he thought that people in the future might not believe it had actually happened. It is not hard to rewrite history. He regarded the museum as a truth bank. But it is not enough to see a video lying on a shelf in a showcase. It is a camera and a cassette – we can see that – and we have to take the museum's word that it belonged to and was used by Gorbachev. But what does that tell us about the truth of his assertion? To begin to judge that, and to share his experience, what visitors need is to see the video played. All too often museums think they have done their job if they show one aspect of the truth, usually the simplest one; but, in truth, they have hardly begun.

Denarius of Tiberius, 14–37 CE. The original Tribute Penny referred to in the Bible
(Matthew 22, 19): 'Render therefore unto Caesar the things that are Caesar's'.
British Museum

CHAPTER THREE

Collections and Collectors

If the aim of museums is to reveal truth, then collections are their means. The question museums have to ask themselves is whether their collections help them achieve this goal. There are as many different collections as there are collectors. But not many collections are of interest to others, and few merit inclusion in a museum. Children commonly gather what they like around them to find out about the world and to help them establish their identity. This can be a private activity, restricted to the child's bedroom, or it can become a very public display, as they barter fiercely with each other to build bigger and better sets; sometimes it is both. David Attenborough described how, as a child of eight, he persuaded the most beautiful woman he had yet seen (Jacquetta Hopkins – who, under her married name, Hawkes, was later to become a distinguished archaeologist) to venture into his room to see his museum of fossils and other natural wonders. He was acting rather like a bowerbird, captured on one of his own nature films, tempting a female into its elaborately decorated nest. The desire to collect can continue beyond puberty, and the motives for doing so can be complex. The wife of William Randolph Hearst, the American newspaper entrepreneur who was the model for Citizen Kane, claimed that her husband collected things when he was in a worried state of mind. If she was right, the spectacular array of art treasures that graced Hearst's home at San Simeon in California, was essentially a visual shield for his insecurity. Though personal and psychological motives weave their secret threads through many museum collections, they have ultimately been gathered together for public benefit and can only be judged by their success in fulfilling that purpose.

In the 18th century, when the doors of the Enlightenment opened, amateur collectors, amongst whom the most famous was Charles Darwin, began scouring the world for artefacts that could reveal hitherto undreamt-of organising principles in the history of mankind and in the formation of nature. Darwin's barnacles, which he studied painstakingly every day for six years, are now slowly disintegrating in drawers in the Natural History Museum. Taxonomy was the process by which major discoveries were made, in cultural as well as natural history. It dominated all fields of museum collecting and still has value in some fields of study, notably natural history, where knowledge of biodiversity has acquired a new urgency as we enter a period of mass extinction, though this will not necessarily lead to collections of material that are suitable for, or even possible to display. A taxonomic approach, when imaginatively directed, can still reveal much about human behaviour. The Gallery of English Costume at Platt Hall in Manchester is founded on a collection gathered together in the 1930s by a doctor, C. Willet Cunnington, who developed a passionate interest in the history of clothing (not costume). He and his wife, who was also a physician, spent their spare time collecting clothes that illustrated technological or social change and mass psychology. Soon they had filled two, 50-foot long huts at the bottom of their garden. Dr Cunnington was particularly interested in underwear. It was rumoured that when visiting patients he would rummage through their drawers saying, 'You won't be wanting this any more'. The private Heatherbank Museum of Social Work was a similarly remarkable enterprise. It was opened in 1975 in Milngavie, just outside Glasgow, by Colin Harvey, who had devoted his life to collecting evidence of how our attitudes to mental and physical disability had changed over the centuries. The modest displays, in two converted living rooms, included highly imaginative, simple interactives to enable visitors to experience some aspects of disability. The museum is now managed by Glasgow Caledonian University, and changing exhibitions are mounted from its collections. Cunnington and Harvey collected things that no one thought to collect before, and by doing so provided new insights into significant aspects of human life that have, until now, been largely ignored. But a taxonomic approach to many aspects of life can lead to a blinkered approach to collecting.

Coin Collections

Most general museums have collections of coins. The British Museum has the world's largest and finest. Coins are eminently collectable; they are small, easily handled, durable, can be attractive to look at, and are obviously worth something, the more so if they are rare and make whole sets. They were originally collected by museums, however, not to accumulate wealth, but because they share a format that invites comparison and, through their inscriptions and decorations, can reveal whole social structures. The British Museum's coin collection helped to provide a chronology for history, a human equivalent of rings on a tree. A period spent in the coin department used to be essential training for any museum curator. Now we have many other ways of dating history. Collecting coins became an end in itself, so much so that the British Museum woke up comparatively late to the fact that they had very little paper money. It was not until the late 1980s that they seriously began to acquire, with the help of several banks, a collection of bank notes, just as, by coincidence, these were losing their primacy as currency, too. The British Museum has now started collecting credit cards. It is still thinking in terms of categories of objects, not the purposes of collecting. Instead of maintaining a Department of Coins and Medals (only a museum could contrive such a conjunction), the British Museum could create a Department of Money, dealing with the whole system of exchange. Coins only really come fully alive when you know what they were worth when in circulation. Jesus' recommendation to render unto Caesar the things that are Caesar's, has little meaning when coins no longer represent a year's labour but have become merely loose change. I have, however, never seen a collection of coins that included items which could have been purchased with them at the time of their currency, though this would be a comparatively easy thing to do. Museums to date have tended to collect the hardware, not the software of life, the product not the purpose. If they want their collections to become meaningful again, museums need to know what their collections meant in the past and what they could mean today.

Industrial museums tend to be full of engines but contain little about what the engines are for. That is fine if one is interested in the development of engines in themselves, but few people are. In the late 1970s, as the steel furnaces closed, Sheffield's Kelham Island Industrial Museum decided to acquire, as a monument to this great industry, the River Don Engine, a vast machine, one of the largest of its type ever built, which was used to drive an armour-plate rolling mill. The engine cost a great deal to move and install in the museum. Then it had to be got into working order, which took over three years. It is an impressive sight, with its gleaming pistons pounding away about 30 feet up in the air. But the deeper understanding of its significance came from the accompanying film of the engine working in the factory. It showed it in the distance, dwarfed by the remarkable scene around it. The engine powered a sea of rollers through which were passing dozens of vast, burning sheets of metal, sliding back and forth, gradually getting thinner and thinner. The steel workers, standing beside these huge, moving, fiery beds of metal, were throwing onto them, every now and then, branches of aspen, which burst into sparks as they hit the almost molten surface. Extraordinarily, among all this technology, aspen twigs had not been bettered as a lubricant. The engine, though impressive, was really peripheral to this amazing process. It might have been just as well if the museum had acquired nothing more than one of the vast sheets of metal laid across rollers, a basket of aspen twigs and the protective clothing of the workers, along with this film. Another plate, standing on end, could give visitors a vivid sense of the size of the battleships that could be built with them, especially if another film showed one in action. So the cycle of meaning could be made complete, and the military effort that funded the whole process made manifest, revealing how marginal, despite its massiveness, the River Don Engine really was.

The curators in Sheffield might object with some justification to this criticism of their collecting policy by arguing that they exist to collect engines, not document wars. But can one collect something because it is big without also considering the reason why it is so big? By imposing limits on their collecting, museums limit their potential to interest their public. Though collecting areas are becoming more intelligently designated, collections are still ring-fenced, and this has a direct effect on the museum's public. The curators at the People's Palace, Glasgow Museums' pioneering social history museum founded in 1898, did not collect material on the history of the workers in the shipbuilding industry, because they maintained this was the job of their colleagues who ran Glasgow's Museum of Transport, where all the shipbuilding material was displayed. The curators in that museum thought it was not their job because they were a technological museum, and that the People's Palace should do it because they collected social history. So neither did so, and this vital aspect of the city's social and cultural life slipped through the net, and the public for this lost history was lost too.

Thinking of its public first, a museum might, instead of buying an early painting by a well-known local artist, acquire paintings by a foreign artist whose work is familiar to a recent group of immigrants. The painting would form a contrast to that of the local painter rather than amplifying his work, and throw light on a different but contemporary tradition. Decisions like these all require shifts in policy, but carrying on doing what one has always done is also a policy decision. A Trabant car exhibited beside a VW Golf, preferably with photographs of their owners, could speak volumes not just about the manufacture of cars, but the whole political economy of the East and West at the moment the Wall came down, yet few transport museums would consider it lay within their remit to collect such a comparison.

Traditionally museums collect one of every type, whether it be a new coin, a credit card, or a different type of engine. The origins of this approach go back to the radical ideas of Aristotle. Learning, he maintained, could be acquired not by listening to others or reading what they had written, but by studying the world around him and trusting the evidence of his own eyes. His pupil, Demetrius of Phalerium, created a museum alongside the library at Alexandria, to help him continue the work his master had begun in

Athens of classifying and co-ordinating all fields of human knowledge. Many people think museums should still be like reference libraries – they only need to get one of everything to have done their job. It is just possible to conceive of a comprehensive collection of all the books in the world, but it is madness to think of a comprehensive collection of objects – of, say, textile designs or of one work by every artist in the world, self-defined or even academically designated. The Dutch government tried to do just that in the 1970s, collecting one work from all artists who graduated from art school. They now have warehouses full of art that no one knows what to do with. The policy has been discontinued.

The German artist Joseph Beuys maintained that everyone was an artist (though, judging by the prices he asked for his works, he clearly thought some are better artists than others). With charming, millennial generosity, the local art gallery of Kerteminde, a small town in Denmark, invited all those who lived in their area and thought they were artists to exhibit. They expected there would be about 50. There were twice that many, 100 out of a population of 10,000. By extrapolation, that makes 70,000 artists in Britain alone. Where does that leave the collecting policies of most galleries of modern art? The vast majority of these artists, it is true, will produce little worthy of wide attention, but a few will be highly original, and a handful will, quite possibly, have something exceptional to offer, which may well not be those the curator already knows. History tells us that art is unpredictable: it can spring up anywhere, like mushrooms from an invisibly extensive mycelium. It is only after the event that we can begin to understand the social and individual circumstances which created the fertile conditions in which the art of a particular age flourished. Art galleries are full of contemporary purchases that reflect what curators at the time thought art *ought* to be, while much of the art we now value was disregarded. Gallery collections are sitting targets for artists concerned with their reputations, while the works of painters like Van Gogh (who committed suicide shortly after he received his first good review) slipped by uncollected.

Jean Tinguely, the Swiss artist whose kinetic machines expressed so much about post-war industrial decline, genetic engineering and our increasingly frenetic society, told in me once that he hated 'shit art venues' and that 'museums were the death of art'. He made sure his art was seen in the streets, where people lived, not incarcerated in museums and galleries. Jim Whiting, the British artist whom Tinguely regarded, in some ways, as his heir, does not work in galleries at all. You have to go to nightclubs in Germany to see his fantastic, elaborate evocations of modern heavens and hells. You would be hard put, too, to see many works in public collections by even an artist as famous as

David Hockney. Most of his paintings are privately owned, and some of his best work was produced, fleetingly, for the theatre. By far the largest public display of his work is in the 1853 Gallery, located in a clothes shop at Salt's Mill, near Bradford. And the most popular living artist in Britain today, Beryl Cook (genuinely popular for her work, that is, not because she is always in the press), was not included in any public collection at all, until the Gallery of Modern Art in Glasgow acquired her work in 1996, much to the disgruntlement of the majority of the art press. Her sin was that her art existed totally outside the circuit of galleries of contemporary art, both public and commercial, which repeatedly promote the same chosen few wherever they can in the world. There will be some lasting art in this incestuous circuit, but museum curators need to take a wider view of visual creativity across the whole spectrum of society, in order to select the art that will continue to have something to say after the marketing boys have moved on. This is no easy task, faced with the plethora of modern production; it takes time to assess lasting qualities and a brave independence from the numerous vested interests that tie their coat-tails to the art world. But it is important work, because so much that could benefit people in future can so easily be lost. Had it not been for the efforts of John Heminge and Henry Condell, who compiled the First Folio, much of Shakespeare's poetry would have melted into thin air.

The Museum of Scotland

When the National Museums of Scotland were preparing to open their new Museum of Scotland, they found that they had extensive holdings from the Bronze Age to the 19th century, but only a patchwork of domestic and industrial artefacts representing the 20th century. The experience of people living in Scotland in modern times had somehow slipped through the net. The Museum's solution was bold but flawed. They invited the people of Scotland themselves to select the items that would illustrate their history. A film clip, a pop song, a political speech, the sound of a news vendor or the school bell could all have been legitimate choices, as long as they were put into a wider and deeper context by the Museum itself. As it was, a fairly random group of Scots, ranging from schoolchildren to celebrities, were invited to select an object of significance to them. So instead of being given personal insights into the great themes of Scottish life in the 20th century, such as the Depression, the two world wars, radical politics, the rise and fall of Utopian rehousing schemes, the rise of nationalism, the cultural renaissance, industrial decline, laughter, alcohol and religion, the visitor is presented with a pot-pourri of personal mementoes that have little wider resonance, such as a bottle of Fairy Liquid because, we are told by its selector, it gets the dishes 'squeaky clean', or a packet of sugar-free sweets that, we are informed, are better for one's teeth. The celebrity's choices are the most banal. A TV presenter chose an open-top Saab because she could drive around in it when she was over 40 without looking silly, while the Prime Minister, Tony Blair, selected a Fender Stratocaster guitar because it reminded him of the time when every teenager wanted to be in a pop group (though I know at least one who wanted to be Prime Minister).

We need to preserve the past not merely for nostalgic reasons. Nostalgia is personal; it dies with each individual and generation. The past only merits preservation if it has something to teach us. The burgeoning of museums about the Holocaust in the 1990s – there are now 12 in the United States alone – has been partly prompted by the fact that we are losing the last generation of its witnesses, but more importantly by the desire not to lose evidence from past events that still have a great deal to teach us. Museums have an urgent responsibility to collect and show the lessons we need to learn from history. A museum of the history of Communism, showing its origins, hopes and ideals, opponents, battles and betrayals, could make a major contribution to world history and understanding, had anyone the courage and means to fund one. Similarly, a museum about apartheid is an urgent necessity before so much of the evidence is lost or fudged. If new institutions cannot be established to deal with subjects of such weight and impact, the museum community as a whole, instead of just sticking to their existing categories of collecting, has to find ways to ensure such evidence is preserved until it can be properly studied and displayed.

Instead of acting solely as a passive receptacle, saying yes or no to the next old mangle, wedding dress or stamp collection, museums need to think much more creatively about what the past could offer the future, and what their role could be in that transaction. The past used to be much more integrated into people's lives, but modern lifestyles tend to erode that relationship. Museums could play a key role in helping to fill that gap. Paradoxical though it may seem, the oldest culture of all has the most profound sense of responsibility for its past. A traditional Aboriginal person's tribal responsibility is to keep his or her designated hill, river or animal alive by dreaming it; that is, by retelling its history in stories, songs, dances and paintings. If they do not go on doing this, they believe, the things themselves, the animals, and even the night sky, will die. This is a much more serious and vital approach to the past than is common in Western society. In the West, museums come closest to fulfilling this sustaining role but the task is usually seen as an institutional, and often a token one; it is rarely regarded as vital. Museums need to create such a living role for the past, as the modern world becomes more uniform in its appearances and practices.

In Western society it is often left to the efforts of inspired individuals to preserve significant parts of our heritage. Bob Edwards, an amateur archaeologist from Adelaide, did much of the pioneering work on the Aboriginal rock carvings of Australia, at a time in the late 1950s and 1960s when there was little interest in them and no one believed that they were as old as they were subsequently shown to be. He persuaded the government to legislate to preserve as many of them as he could, but soon realised that he had to help the Aboriginal people to preserve their culture as well. He played a key role in channelling the government's arts programme to help Aboriginal culture to survive. A programme that paid the Aboriginal people to paint meant buyers had to be found for their work. The situation rapidly became difficult; the Government were amassing works of art that no one at that time was interested in acquiring. The solution was to organise major exhibitions abroad that generated first international, then local, respect for Aboriginal culture. This turnaround had been achieved by the confluence of two quite different artistic traditions, an unlikely marriage brokered by people within Aboriginal and Western European culture, who shared a belief in the importance of preserving the past. The recently opened National Museum of Australia in Canberra is the result of nearly 30 years of campaigning and adroit political manoeuvring on Bob Edwards' part.

Many museum collections today started life as private passions, not all of which merit a public lifeline. When money is involved, motives can get mixed. Not only can collecting antiques in itself be an investment, but the process of putting things together in a way that enhances their significance, what is called 'building a collection', can in itself add considerable value to each item. This is true of sets of domestic objects and even more so of works of art; fortunes can be made. In the United States, it is common practice for a wealthy individual to spend time building collections of early photographs, Chinese bronzes, medieval manuscripts, Persian rugs or contemporary paintings, frequently with the help and advice of a museum curator. He or she may also have the good fortune and contacts to get onto a museum board, where such help is easily available. The collector then gives or sells his collection to the museum when tax advantages are at their most favourable, often on the condition that the collection is kept together. The result is that American museums, today, can be a patchwork of individual benefactions, which may be difficult to integrate. The Art Institute of Chicago has expanded eight-fold since its foundation in 1879 and in the process has become one of the easiest museums in the world to get lost in both mentally and physically, which is quite an achievement. You walk up over bridges, down stairs, round corners, through galleries, across courtyards until you have no idea where you are or how to get back to where you were. Successive benefactors have each demanded that a new gallery be built to immortalise their gifts of Impressionist paintings or modern art, colonial American furniture or archaic Chinese jades, arms and armour or antique glass, prints and drawings or paperweights. It is now very difficult to hold in one's mind what the Art Institute of Chicago is, or what it might want to become.

Private collectors are not necessarily good museum collectors, even when they are very rich. Sir William Burrell made his fortune in buying, managing and selling ships in Glasgow at a time when half the ships afloat in the world were built along the banks of the Clyde. He turned this fortune into art; into nearly 9,000 objects ranging from works by Rembrandt and Degas to medieval tapestries and Sung porcelain. Burrell, as far as one can tell from the few records left, was not in the habit of expressing emotion. Perhaps this accounts for his endless search for beautiful things. He welcomed visitors and praise not for himself, but for his collection, which was to be his monument and was, perhaps, a substitute for conventional relationships. His wife, evidently, hated it. Despite the airiness of the Gallery that now houses the collection, with its views onto the surrounding woodland, and the sheer beauty of many of the exhibits, the overall effect tends to heaviness, as if something of Burrell's oppressive obsession has survived. When his collection arrived in Glasgow, many of the items were still wrapped in the packaging in which they were sent to him from his dealers. It was as if the act of collecting was enough; once acquired Burrell did not want to look at them again. Rich people who bequeath their collections to the public usually do so, at least in part, to immortalise themselves. J. Paul Getty never even visited his museum at Malibu, but who wants to visit his own tomb? Even the beautiful Frick Collection in New York has a whiff of the graveyard about it. Museums have to be for the living.

Many collections are made for visual effect, even when their main intentions are scientific, to illustrate, for example, the biodiversity of a given environment. Naturalists have to be visually acute, and they train themselves to see details most people would not notice. Moths have never been so popular as butterflies, so it is only recently that some rarer species have been protected, and collections of moths for scientific study are still being made; row upon row of spread-eagled specimens pinned to boards in glass-topped drawers. One naturalist told me how the criteria for these collections varied: one collector insisted on always having five specimens of each species; another only wanted immaculate specimens and therefore did not collect the moths themselves but their caterpillars, which he reared, killing the moth immediately it emerged; another collected specimens from the wild, whether they were battered or not, because he was interested in the wear and tear caused by a particular life and habitat. They all disapproved of those who bought specimens, missing the thrill of seeing the creatures alive. And of course, they all condemned those who bought specimens just to sell them again. But whatever their motive, the appearance of their collections was important, and added crucially to their satisfaction and sense of achievement.

In his collection of dialogues, *Oeconomicus*, the Greek historian Xenophon describes how his master, Socrates, asserted that even objects which were of little interest individually, could look good when arranged together. The example he gave was Phoenician pots, which were then two a penny. The repetition of their contours creates a harmony, like the ordered rows of identical columns on Greek temples, which expresses an ideal relationship between mankind, the world and the gods. (The classical portico became identified with museums in the 18th century and has remained their international symbol to this day.) Appearances, however, can be misleading. I remember a man in Venice explaining why he had amassed a large collection of coffee tins. The first cup of coffee in the morning was, for him, the same as waking up to a new day. It was a time he treasured, and he could not bear to throw away the tins which contained the beans that triggered this experience. Nobody else, seeing the attractive array of brightly coloured tins piled on shelves by the hundred, would conjure up a joyous sequence of Venetian dawns.

Kettle's Yard

Jim Ede's collection, now at Kettle's Yard, Cambridge, was created purely for its visual effect. Here the accumulative effect is one of light. Ede built up his collection while he was a curator at the Tate Gallery in London. He acquired what the Tate did not want, particularly the work of the modern artists of the St Ives school; the short-lived sculptor, Henri Gaudier-Brzeska; the mystical Welsh painter-poet, David Jones; and the naive artist, Alfred Wallis, who painted evocations of the sea on scraps of card as a way of keeping himself company after his wife's death. Ede arranged the works around and about the rambling half-timbered cottage where he lived in Cambridge. He loved light, and it is memories of light that you take away with you when you leave his cottage, now preserved by Cambridge University – light falling on a spiral of white pebbles, declining in size, placed on a weathered oak table under a window; light falling across an uneven floor with a few rugs thrown across it; light on a jug of flowers, in the half shade behind a curtain; light from an old, silvered mirror throwing reflections into a darker corner; and light, above all, glowing out from the pictures on the walls. The art here is part of an encompassing sensibility that nevertheless allows each work to speak individually. Ede expressed himself by collecting, arranging and illuminating the work of others, and his museum has merit because of that.

All museums have certain objects that work brilliantly in an exhibition. These are usually on permanent display, and feature most often in the museum's literature; they are the 'must-see' objects that give the museum its identity. Most museums also have many objects that have little visual appeal and can rarely, if ever, be used in a display, yet they may be interesting to a researcher. If a museum emphasised only its exhibition role, it would be tempted to dispose of specialist material. But if it has an archival function as well, it develops such collections with scholarship in mind. Curators working on research have a great deal to learn from archivists. By learning to work together, archivists and museum curators would become much more effective at preserving their heritage. Archivists currently have to keep abreast of intellectual developments on a very broad front in a way that most curators do not. They have to be aware, too, that research interests are changing. The Minnesota History Centre began collecting records of the multi-national companies that had their headquarters in the state. They soon began to realise that they also needed to collect the social policies of these organisations. As they looked further, they realised the potential for collecting records of managerial change. The history of management is a comparatively new discipline but the Minnesota History Centre, through its foresight, has been able to provide an excellent basis for the study of this subject.

The Minnesota History Centre

The Minnesota History Centre, in St Paul, is based on the collections of the Minnesota Historical Society, one of many such organisations founded across the United States by enthusiastic amateurs, mostly in the 19th century, to preserve all aspects of local history. Their functions had largely been superseded by state-funded institutions such as museums, libraries, archives and public record offices, and many had dwindled to the point of extinction by the end of the 20th century. While the New-York Historical Society, one of the oldest, was selling off works from its collection to stay afloat, the Minnesota History Centre combined all its archive and museum material alongside video and sound recordings, and all government records, to become a major focal point for the whole community. It looks and feels like a modern cathedral. Opened in 1992 at a cost of $110 million, its towering multicoloured granite halls teem with activity, school parties, weddings, political meetings, tourists, researchers, conferences and all manner of local performances. It is a remarkable declaration of public support for the role that history can play in our lives.

Yet, though the past has been united, its management has not. Its archival and museum functions are still run separately. Archivists are used to acting quickly. They may only have weeks, sometimes days, to preserve the records of a business that is about to go bankrupt. They are used to making broad decisions about the potential research significance of the material available. They then fine-tune the acquisition later. Museum curators are used to dotting every 'i' and crossing every 't' before an acquisition is made. To them, once an object enters the collection it becomes sacred. It therefore has to be fully researched, classified, and assessed by conservators before it can be given an accession number. In Minnesota, where entire businesses are collected including products as well as records and processes, the museum curator can still be deciding how to classify these or assess their items when the liquidator arrives.

Archivists make a distinction between natural and artificial collections, a policy that could be usefully applied to museums as a whole. A collection of records accumulated by a business as part of its working practice would be defined as natural, whereas a collection of old masters or beer mats would be regarded as artificial. At first, the majority of museum collections would seem to fall into the artificial category, simply because they have been acquired for display. But certain aspects of museum collections are better defined as natural because they have been acquired as part of a systematic piece of research. Collections of the flora and fauna made during a study of biodiversity, or the remains found during an archaeological dig, or even a comprehensive collection of artist's prints to facilitate authentication of works by his hand, are natural collections, and therefore archival by nature. It is informative to apply this 'natural' category to collections acquired by museums for display, to identify their purpose. Many art collections, both now and in the past, have been made to illustrate a point; either to display the owner's wealth or taste or, more interestingly, to illustrate art history, or to promote a particular aesthetic or moral standpoint. Display collections inevitably reflect the concerns and social values of their times. If, in the future, a curator's passionate and partial collecting for the present ceases to be of widespread interest but becomes merely a study collection for future students of those times, so be it. Nobody can predict what will be valued in the future, or how posterity will view the achievements of their age.

A museum might have under consideration the acquisition of, say, a complete set of horse's armour, an early painting by a well-known local artist, or an engine that demonstrates a key stage in the development of the motor car, because these might enhance the museum's professional reputation and educational significance. If the museum engages in that purchase, however, it forgoes some other expenditure. Perhaps, instead of acquiring the horse's armour, although it may look splendid and complement suits of armour that the museum already possesses, the museum could instead re-deploy its existing collection in a fresh way. It might create a context of pageantry and of the symbolic struggle between good and evil, for which much armour was originally used, and not, as many visitors immediately assume, on the battlefield. Perhaps, in this context, they could more usefully acquire a set of costumes from *Star Wars*, which owe their form and design to the type of armour on display. Such an approach might not attract the specialists or enthusiasts but it might interest a new generation of visitors, even without the benefit of the equestrian set, and lead them to an understanding of the historical pieces of armour. Newly interested visitors might then be prompted to visit other armoury museums or even generate funds for further purchases. Curators collecting works for contemporary display can afford to be more partial than archivists. A commitment to making collections that have meaning for us today might prove, in time, the best way of ensuring that museums enjoy a profound future.

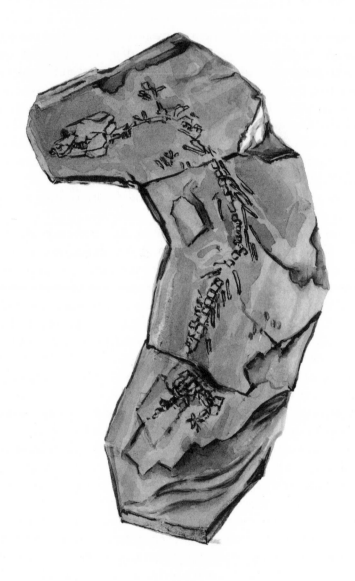

'Lizzie', *Westlothiana Lizziae*, first (or holotype) fossil specimen of a lizard
or amphibian (male or female), 338 million years old.
Museum of Scotland

CHAPTER FOUR

With or Without Objects

The curators' refrain is that their collections are everything. But if collections are a means to an end, not an end in themselves, do museums necessarily need them? Are objects, anyway, not too obdurate and cumbersome to communicate many subtleties of meaning? Why have a stuffed tiger in a case when you can show a video of one running? Can looking at an internal combustion engine, stilled in a display case, inspire one to think about man's appetite for speed, let alone the impact of pollution? If a museum wants to tackle such issues, would it not be better to go directly to the subject and only use objects if there is no better way of illustrating a point?

Though the caricature of a museum – as a place where old things go to gather dust – still holds sway to some degree in the popular imagination, many museums have, in the last few decades, changed out of all recognition. Some contain hardly any objects at all, relying more on interactive, dramatic displays than they do on genuine objects. These museums have been influenced by developments in the 1960s and 1970s, which saw science and heritage centres and children's museums discover radical ways of interesting large numbers of people in subjects that were traditionally the domain of museums, but without using collections at all. Since then, a gulf has opened between those museums which value these new approaches and those that want to maintain the primacy of their collections. It is essentially a battle over whether a museum is there to preserve the past or to educate its audience through entertainment. This is a rift that can be healed, however, because the intentions of these educational attractions are often profoundly serious, their methods highly imaginative and effective. They have much to teach traditional museums. Indeed, if museums do not learn from them, they could easily become marginalised by society, their collections relegated to outlying stores while theme-park installations take centre stage.

The visitor attractions that now rival museums grew from within museums themselves. They sprung from the inspiration of three outstanding museum entrepreneurs: Michael Spock at the Children's Museum, Boston, Frank Oppenheimer at the Exploratorium in San Francisco and Jeshajahu Weinberg at the Museum of the Jewish Diaspora in Tel Aviv. All three felt frustrated by the difficulties museums faced in reaching new audiences. They leapfrogged the restraints of conventional museum thinking simply by doing without the collections, and found themselves free to develop whole new vocabularies of communication.

The Children's Museum, Boston

Michael Spock, the son of the childcare expert, Dr Benjamin Spock, conceived his Children's Museum in Boston, Massachusetts, from the child's point of view. He asked the simple question: what are children interested in? The answer was the world of grown ups. Most of the collections held by children's museums did not supply this need at all. They were actually for adults: antique toys triggered adult memories but held little meaning for modern-day children. Toys are for playing with, as every child knows, which is the one thing one cannot do with old and valuable toys. Michael Spock realised that children in museums want to play, above all to play at being grown up. Conventional children's museums were about children and for adults rather than being for children and about adults. At Boston, Spock put all the collections aside, leaving one large showcase at the entrance to show what the displays used to look like – a museum of the museum. The rest of the multi-storey space he filled with interactive exhibits, staffed by guides, not guards (many of them, over time, selected from visitors who had grown up with the museum). These guides were trained to encourage children to use them to find out about the world around them; how a sewage system functioned, for instance, or what it might be like to work in a factory. There were collectable objects in this museum, like a clocking-in machine and a plumbing system, but all were there to be played with and used.

When the museum did a display about Japan, they asked American children what they would like to know about Japanese children. This led them to reconstruct a typical Japanese children's bedroom, containing everything needed by the three kids of different ages who shared it. This display was presented as *son et lumière*, with the voice of each child in turn pointing out his or her possessions, telling you what each meant to them; for example, where their beds were – futons rolled up and stored in the base of the cupboards during the day. The youngest child's fighting monsters jerked into life when they were illuminated, and were soon locked in battle. Hanging from one slightly open cupboard door was a cat's tail, which swished back and forth when its turn came to take part in the tale of this highly organised but hectic bedroom – an unforgettable glimpse into the private, everyday world of three kids who lived on the opposite side of the globe.

The Children's Museum in Boston has inspired countless similar institutions around the world, but few have managed to emulate its invigorating, experimental spirit. The Exploratorium in San Francisco has, if anything, been even more slavishly replicated. The attractions it contains derive from the inventions that Frank Oppenheimer and his team made there during the 1970s and early 1980s. Frank was the brother of Robert, the atomic physicist who later opposed the use and proliferation of nuclear weapons. Frank devoted his life's work to popular education. The more we understand about science, he believed, the more we will be able to control it.

The Exploratorium, San Francisco

During a year spent visiting museums in Europe, Frank Oppenheimer saw, at the Science Museum in London, an extremely popular basement display of simple interactive exhibits. These had been developed out of much earlier scientific demonstrations dating from the 18th century, which were still in the museum's collection (there is not much that is new under the sun). Oppenheimer realised that it would be possible to make a quantum leap in this interactive approach by using modern technology. In developing his ideas, Oppenheimer was strongly influenced by a remarkable man he met in Israel, who had devised the world's first modern, interactive science display in 1964, temporarily housed in a disused British barracks in Tel Aviv. Ivan Moscovich had survived Auschwitz and Bergen Belsen as a young man of 17, ultimately by lying on a pile of corpses for almost a week, lucky enough to still be alive when the camp was liberated. He came to believe that the most effective counter to mankind's potential for cruelty was the development of our ability to play. Moscovich devoted his life to inventing puzzles and games, and a series of interactive toys that enabled the user to understand scientific and mathematical principles. Many of these were incorporated by Frank Oppenheimer into his Exploratorium that eventually opened in 1969 in an architectural folly. The principle behind the Exploratorium is the same as that behind the Boston Children's Museum; one is not shown how something works, but discovers it for oneself.

The San Francisco Palace of Fine Arts, built in 1915, is a great arc of a building graced with colossal statues of gods and goddesses. A more unlikely venue for a modern science museum would be hard to imagine, but inside it is a vast, uncluttered dark space, ideal for Oppenheimer's purposes. Upon entering, one of the first things to be seen is a large workshop, behind an open-mesh screen, where new ideas for displays are being developed by scientists, artists and amateur enthusiasts who work there on grants awarded by the Exploratorium. Here they build and test new interactive devices, all in the public eye. The atmosphere in the place – the sense of experimentation and participation – is electric. The attractions in this museum are not rare objects, but the excitement generated by people discovering and understanding processes. Virtually the whole menu of interactive exhibits that have become such a familiar sight in science centres around the world, were developed here over a period of 20 years, in an atmosphere of creative collaboration within the dark, curving space of the Exploratorium.

While the Exploratorium and the Childrens' Museum in Boston were being established, a parallel development was taking place in history museums. In 1968, Jeshajahu Weinberg, a theatre director in Tel Aviv, was invited to create a museum about the Jewish Diaspora. But there were no collections that recorded this story; in the many places around the world where the Jewish people have settled, they were either not allowed to manifest their presence or their traces were eradicated. Theirs was an invisible history. But Weinberg was not deterred: he knew he had an important and powerful story to tell, and he resolved to find a way of doing so, even without relics from the past. As he would have done in the theatre, he immediately set about appointing a designer to help to develop the concept. He chose the Englishman James Gardner, who had been working as an exhibition designer since 1938. Together they generated virtually the whole menu of object-less storytelling techniques that have now become so familiar in heritage centres: reconstructed tableaux, models, moving light shows, life-size replicas, film sequences, audio booths, commissions from artists, even cartoons. For the first time, a museum incorporated booths with computers (then still a novelty), so that visitors who wanted to find out more information about their place in Jewish history could do so. These were situated so that they could be used without interrupting the main narrative flow of the museum. The great contribution of Weinberg and Gardner was to develop the art of telling stories through exhibitions. They made astute judgments about how much they could expect each visitor to absorb at each stage in the display, when to let the visitors rest and when to stimulate their attention. To illustrate the proliferation of Jewish communities throughout the world, they had the idea, which appears simple in hindsight, of commissioning dozens of models of synagogues from around the world. These showed how the Jews adopted the external architectural styles and cultures of the countries in which they settled, from Chicago to China to Venice, while the interiors, which were exposed on one side, remain notably consistent. You get the idea immediately you walk into this extraordinary, vast gallery.

The Museum of the Jewish Diaspora, Tel Aviv

The Museum of the Jewish Diaspora begins dramatically as you enter, with a tumbling row of vast blocks of stone, exact replicas of those used to build the Temple in Jerusalem, which was destroyed in 70 CE, an event that signalled the beginning of the Jewish Diaspora of our era. The visitor then turns a corner and is confronted with another pile of blocks, this time in the form of numerous screens showing the different faces of Jewish people living today in all the corners of the world, of every racial type and mode of dress. Visitors grasp, within the first few steps they take, what the museum is about, its beginning and its end. Then it proceeds to tell its visitors what happened in between.

On the whole, this is a positive and, at times, celebratory story of human survival, but at the heart of the museum, in the centre of the staircase that takes one up through layer after layer of history, is a dark well. Hung in the centre of this black, empty space and rising, seemingly endlessly, into the darkness above, is a four-sided, black-barred portcullis. Inside this is suspended a 'pillar of fire', made up of a myriad of small light bulbs. A large text on the wall, at the foot of this stairwell, reminds the visitor of the many people who have died for their beliefs throughout the history of the Jewish people. This is the earliest example I know of a museum using an artistic installation to express a key idea and communicate feeling. It does so very powerfully. You come across this well of suffering and hope as you rise, floor by floor, through the museum. On the top floor of the museum, however, this sacrificial column stops at eye level, just short of the ceiling. The implication is that the age of repression is finally over. Then you enter the last phase of the display. For the first time, the floor under you slopes upwards and you exit through a display praising the new state of Israel. The museum ends as propaganda.

Many curators in traditional museums regarded the initiatives exemplified by these three museums with suspicion. They felt that they implicitly undermined the very essence of their museums' existence, the need for their collections. Some curators reacted by making their museums more museum-like than they had ever been before. They brought everything they could out of storage to create new 'cabinets of curiosities', packed with fascinating things, all traditionally labelled, without an interactive technique or a reproduction in sight. In Britain, Manchester City Art Gallery led the way by restoring its galleries to their 'original splendour'. The curators scoured the archives for early pictures of the interiors and conservators took paint scrapes of the walls to determine the first colour schemes. As many pictures as possible were taken from the stores and hung from floor to ceiling on dark, damask walls. Period showcases were restored, borrowed, bought or replicated, and filled with *objets d'art*. One of the drawbacks of this approach is that such displays tend to become fixed and are difficult to change. Even more seriously, pinning everything to one earlier period obliterates the traces of other uses and attitudes to art that the gallery might have adopted through time. Public galleries need a degree of anonymity in their ambience to allow for multiple and changing occupancy, boring as this may sound. They cannot thrive if they are set in one period.

The approach of authentic recreation may be argued to have validity when one is displaying a period home. But even then, changes over time have their place in any attempt at reconstruction. At Temple Newsam House near Leeds, the curators have recreated an interior in which the original owners would have felt at ease. The building formerly housed a conventional decorative arts museum, which showed the history of design over the centuries. In the 1980s, the new team decided to make the house itself the prime exhibit. Through diligent research into the history of the family and the house over the last four centuries, the curators have been able to trace, replace or reconstruct original furnishings, fittings and decorative schemes. What makes their efforts exceptional is that they have not tried to restore the house to a single period, or used it to exemplify good taste or even typical taste. They have restored its history, with all its natural illogicality, so that one walks from a late Victorian room through to an 18th-century one, and then on to a Victorian one again. The curators have been intelligently pragmatic about their work. It would have been too dangerous to light the Picture Gallery with candles in the process of restoring it to its appearance of 1746, so they chose to add a safer but equally authentic lighting system, installed later in 1894. Visitors often find the house rather off-putting. Many complain about the gloominess of the atmosphere and the garishness of some of the wallpaper. This shows that the restoration is working. Walking through this house, one imagines that one could, at any moment, encounter one of its past owners coming round the corner with his dogs. One feels as though one were a trespasser. Few period reconstructions achieve such a degree of authentic discomfort; most, for understandable economic reasons, want to make visitors feel welcome. The chances are, if we could travel back in time, we would not be. Temple Newsam House is a rare instance of such an authentic reconstruction.

Anchoring a museum in a single period in history limits its capacity to respond to its own age. Such 'authentic' museum interiors might be superficially impressive, but they sacrifice the visitor's individual experience in the interests of creating an overall visual effect. While giving evidence to the Commission appointed to determine the site and contents of the new National Gallery in London in 1857, John Ruskin was asked if he approved of the way the famous Tribune gallery in Florence was arranged, with pictures hung from floor to ceiling. 'No', he replied, 'I think it is merely arranged for show, for showing how many of each thing can be got together'. He believed that pictures should be seen on a level with the eye and added, 'It is not well to have a noble picture many feet above the eye, merely for the glory of the room'. As Ruskin saw it, the visitor's appreciation of each work of art was more important than his appreciation of the museum environment. This could be dismissed as merely being the difference between a Puritan or Catholic approach (Ruskin after all was brought up as a strict Protestant), were it not for the fact that no artist to my knowledge paints pictures to enhance the overall effect of a gallery. If their art was meant for galleries at all, they would have preferred their work to be hung 'on the line', the most sought-after position on the wall of any salon or academy, only allocated to those pictures that the judges thought merited examination without bending or stretching. Looking back on this fashion for reconstructing period museum interiors in the National Gallery of Scotland in Edinburgh, the Walker Art Gallery in Liverpool, and in Cartwright Hall in Bradford (to name three in Britain alone), future generations will probably not see the results as products of an age to which museum curators aspire, but as evidence of these same curators' lack of confidence in the role that museums and galleries can play in people's lives today.

A good reason for putting as much as possible of a collection out on show is to enable more people to have a chance to see more things. But what benefits do these sights bring? Bewildered glances and vacant stares, even when numbered in millions, only indicate a museum's failure to communicate. Rapt individual attention leading to understanding is the only true signal of a museum's success. Many museums give up any attempt to achieve this when faced with hordes of sightseers coming through their doors. A Russian acquaintance of mine told me that when she was ten years old she had cut out a very poor reproduction of the *Mona Lisa* from her mother's copy of *The Female Collective Farm Workers' Magazine*. She knew nothing about art or about Leonardo but something about the picture caught her imagination; it was simple – the lady was smiling. She pinned the picture to the wall beside her bed. Years later, when she came to live in Europe, she discovered that the picture was famous and went to the Louvre to see it. She had only just found it when a tide of guided tourists flooded through and swept her away.

It would be a real diminution of our cultural heritage if pressure of numbers resulted in everyone having to make do with reproductions – as has been the case for years at the Albertina in Vienna, where visitors have to make do with seeing photographs of their famous collection of Dürer drawings – while only scholars and people with connections gain access to the real things. Actually, the problem is exaggerated, and crowd pressure is very much the exception rather than the rule in museums. A popular misconception has grown up in recent years, mainly among those who visit only major tourist attractions or blockbuster exhibitions, that museums everywhere are becoming swamped with tourists. Even in the Louvre, one can walk for miles, enjoying undisturbed views of everything one wants to see; it is only in front of the most famous objects (and there are precious few of these) that the bottlenecks occur. The Louvre, like most of the museums and galleries in the world, is not by any means operating to capacity. In 1996, it attracted just over four-and-a-half million visitors. In the same year, the National Gallery in London, though only a quarter of its size, managed to provide five million visitors with enjoyable and rewarding aesthetic experiences. The Louvre could quite possibly cope with four times its visitor numbers and still not be full. The challenge of giving all its visitors a rewarding experience is one that the Louvre should welcome rather than avoid. It is perfectly possible to ensure that visitors get the most out of seeing the *Mona Lisa* for the first time, standing, while people who have booked to study it for longer could sit beneath their line of vision. Disney World manages millions more people every year than the Louvre, and they have nothing to equal the *Mona Lisa*. Extending opening hours and introducing better crowd management, for a start, would ensure the daughter of the female collective farm worker enjoys to the full her first sight of the actual picture that hung by her bed for so long. It is difficult to imagine a time when people will not want to see the *Mona Lisa*, especially if its extraordinary achievement is much better explained. Nor is it possible to imagine a time when people will be content merely to look at a reproduction, even if it is full size, on a screen at home.

If you can browse through a museum's collections on screen, whether they are on exhibition or in storage, and closely inspect in three dimensions, say, an 18th-century Venetian wine glass, as thin and soft as silk, turn it around as if it were in your hand, and access all the information you want about it without leaving home, you might well feel you never need to visit a museum. Since displaying unique treasures to visitors always exposes them to risk, many conservators and curators would sigh with relief at the thought that, while their objects were being explored by means of a computer, they were in reality tucked up safely in storage. If your aim is to preserve your collections for the future, you are bound to be happy with virtual access at one remove from the rarities themselves. Any access to an object can cause damage, if ever so infinitesimal. Even light is now seen not as the gift of illumination, but as a destructive force to be kept at bay at all costs, hence the off-putting gloom of many galleries today. Virtual access seems to be the answer to all these worries, but it could spell the end of museums and the revelatory experiences that only they can offer. As virtual databases become more widely accessible, the onus will be on museums themselves to prove the benefits of people seeing real things with their own eyes.

Computers need not be seen as the enemy of museums, but rather as a new tool for the museums to use. Computers enable us to look at things in different ways. When all the world's major collections are accessible through a computer, which they will be before too long, anyone will be able to follow their own chain of ideas, rather than having themes imposed on them by others, who include museum staff. One might start by looking at a computer image of a plant specimen in a herbarium, and find oneself going on to study the sexual symbolism of peonies in Chinese porcelain. The associations may be shallow, but they could equally well be profound and lead to discoveries between fields that were previously kept academically separate. Museums will have to create displays that respond to the fresh, interdisciplinary interests that computer access is bound to provoke. The breaking down of existing categories may attach new and unanticipated significance to existing collections. Preparing for the possibility of changes in interest is an inherent part of any museum's task. Those who collected the flora and fauna of New Guinea in the 19th century could not have known that their specimens would be used to study global warming. A collection of majolica made to chart the history of ceramics may reveal to us a great deal about the practice of medicine in the Renaissance. Our museums are treasure-houses of knowledge that could once only be entered through one door and whose contents could be seen from only one angle. Now, all sorts of new vistas are opening up. Computers will not provide a substitute for the museum experience, but encourage more people to want to see real things for themselves. When the Tate Gallery put its collections onto the worldwide web, it had an astonishing 66 million hits in its first year. It is too early to tell whether any of these virtual visitors translate into actual ones, but it would be odd indeed if all this interest led to a fall in visitor numbers at the sites themselves. On the worldwide web, a global museum is growing daily, creating new audiences for museums and challenging them to offer something that it cannot.

Non-collection attractions are also threatened by the development of virtual technology. Why visit children's museums and science centres when you can play many of their games on your computer at home, as is becoming increasingly the case? If you can walk into a virtual simulation of the past, why visit a three-dimensional reconstruction in a heritage park? These educational attractions will need to emphasise what makes them special, as historical entertainment in cyberspace gains pace. One way for them to do this will be to base their displays around unique objects, whether they are to be handled or just looked at. So the two sides of the museum profession could well begin to come together again. They are worlds apart at present.

The Natural History Museum in London has introduced a series of ground-breaking interactive displays that use virtually no objects at all. These are immensely successful; you can hear the din of children enjoying themselves down the corridor as you approach. In one gallery about bugs, though there are barely a couple of dozen real specimens on display among all the levers, models and computers, the place is packed with people. Yet a couple of minutes away you can walk into another gallery which contains literally thousands of specimens, ranging from a stuffed deer to the tiniest beetle, smaller than the pin-head that secures the text beside it, each object carefully selected to show the whole ecology of a particular district, and it is totally devoid of people, except for an attendant.

The same split can be seen in the Field Museum of Natural History in Chicago. During the 1980s, this museum attracted Michael Spock away from his Children's Museum in Boston, to transform their vast acres of displays about ethnology and natural history. His policy was to tell stories, not just show things. One result can be seen in their treatment of life in modern Africa, which is a model of a narrative museum display, using sets and videos and simple interactives, as well as a few carefully chosen real objects. You can sit in half a real African bus and watch life go by on the streets by means of a video. But many curators wanted more money spent on their research and promoting that to the public. Financial problems forced the directorate to decide between the curators and the exhibitors, and Spock had to go. One can still see where he and his team left off their process of transformation. Leaving an interactive display busy with people, one turns a corner to find oneself in a dark, silent gallery, empty except for a guard, with row upon row of dimly lit showcases containing magnificent, magnified models of plants, some segmented to show their inner structure, each immaculately labelled, mostly in Latin. New museums that use their collections imaginatively are having a troubled birth; the collection is either swept away entirely in the modernisation programme, or barricaded in by curators wishing to preserve the museum as it was in the past.

The Asian Civilizations Museum and Tang Dynasty City, Singapore

The Asian Civilizations Museum in Singapore presents the arts and cultures of the East in conventional and immaculate displays of original artefacts. One wing of the museum is devoted to Chinese culture. Tang Dynasty City, beside a highway in the suburbs, is promoted as an educational entertainment for everyone. Within an enclosure surrounded by a replica of a section from the Great Wall of China, 85 Chinese craftsmen have attempted to recreate, at a cost of £40 million, an 8th-century city, complete with temples, a pagoda, a house of pleasure, a tavern, a courthouse, a bank, a library and shops. We are assured, as we are driven round in a toy train, that all the materials and techniques used in the construction are authentic for the Tang Dynasty (618–907 CE). There are no nails, for example, and the timberwork on the two-storey, wooden-framed buildings is generally of high quality. But the illusion of antiquity is undermined at every turn. Plastic bin-liners protrude from Tang Dynasty waste-paper bins, fluorescent tubes dangle above dragon doorways and bright pink drink-vending machines nestle under painted wooden staircases.

Both the Asian Civilizations Museum and the Tang Dynasty City theme park have displays that touch on the extraordinary public examination system which dominated Chinese culture for more than a millennium and made it, in so many ways, unique. Amongst the countless exhibits placed in rows in glass cases in the museum, is a little 18th-century cup decorated with a heron standing among reeds and lotus flowers. The label informs us, in minute print, that the decoration is a verbal pun. In Chinese, the characters for the heron, lotus and reed make up the phrase, 'passing a series of public examinations in consecutive years'. The cup is not part of a display detailing the history of Chinese ceramics, but one about homophonic symbolism. This is a step towards meaning, but it is still a long way from the interests of the general visitor; more people are interested in what puns mean than in the concept of punning itself. In the reconstructed library down a side street in Tang Dynasty City, laid out on trestle tables, are row upon row of fake black volumes, tied with ribbons. A label tells you, in big bold capital letters, that a young man would have had to learn the contents of all these books by heart in order to pass his exams. But neither explains the significance of this system, or the fact that thousands upon thousands of lives hung, every year, on its results.

Public examinations were formalised during the Tang Dynasty and remained in use until 1905, when the Emperor decreed that, if his country was to survive into the 20th century, the administrators of China would need to study science, technology and modern warfare, not just the Confucian Classics, which had been compiled mainly in the 5th century BCE. The enormous impact this system had on individual lives, and on the momentum of a whole culture, could be much more tellingly expressed if the theme park's rows of fake books were piled up as a towering background to the tiny cup; the latter's lovingly painted decoration, the heron stalking among the lotus blossoms and the reeds, would then be invested with so much more meaning. It could become a symbol of hope and freedom after mind-wearying labour, a summer of ease after the exams are over and the dream of a long life beyond them; of social esteem, a happy marriage and long-lasting wellbeing. We could then glimpse the wishes of one young human life, lived long ago, as he raised to his lips this little cup.

The divisions between theme parks and museums seem at present to be growing even further apart. Two new publicly funded, multi-million pound educational attractions have recently opened in Edinburgh, both telling the story of the history of the Earth. In the new Museum of Scotland, a display charts the history of the land that is now Scotland, by means of what is effectively a book on the wall illustrated with dozens of specimens. It begins with the cooling of the Earth's crust and the creation of the continents, and continues through the emergence of life and the subsequent ice ages, as the land mass shifted around the globe from the Antarctic, to where it is today. No visitor I know would have the patience or commitment, or feel the need to absorb all the information in this display. Our Dynamic Earth, on the other hand, deals with the story in terms of elementary banality. Its visitors are herded through a sequence of bays that illustrate the cooling of the earth's surface (the ground shakes), an ice age (a simulated flight over glaciers) and the origins of life (a dinosaur's foot is suspended as if it had just broken through the ceiling). Both make virtually no use of the presence of two remarkable, real things that could have given their visitors memorable experiences, unique in world terms.

The Museum of Scotland includes in its collection the fossil, affectionately called Lizzie, of the oldest lizard or amphibian discovered in the world. She was found in 1984, in a quarry just outside Edinburgh, and all the textbooks of evolution then had to be rewritten. Scotland can stake a claim to be the first place that we have evidence for animals walking on land (a bigger step for mankind). But most visitors to the Museum of Scotland miss the significance of this dark little rock slither, if they notice it at all, because it is tucked round a corner up a cul-de-sac in the display, which is surprising as the museum bought the fossil for the then record sum of £200,000.

Our Dynamic Earth is sited at the foot of Arthur's Seat, the mountain in the centre of Edinburgh that gives the city its famous skyline. This mountain is the remains of a volcano that was active when the land mass that is now called Scotland was a beach on the Equator, and a sea divided it from the land that is now England. Moreover this mountain is of world importance, because it was here that James Hutton discovered rock formations that helped him realise that the world was much, much older that anyone had previously thought, and had been slowly formed over time, not created at one go, and was still changing. Yet visitors leave Our Dynamic Earth without giving the mountain towering above them a second glance, let alone realising its manifold significance in the story they have just been told. Our Dynamic Earth does include a passing reference to Lizzie, represented as a grey model on a grey rock, presumably so as not to upset the overall design. The Museum of Scotland does make something of Arthur's Seat; you can see its lowering mass through a picture window on the roof garden. But had these projects been developed together, what a unique story they could have told! Lizzie walked on Earth within sight of Arthur's Seat when it was a live volcano. Ways have to be found that combine the popular reach of the theme park with the scholarly approach of the museum to bring the past, as it actually happened, vividly to life.

If museums could apply the highly entertaining, often inspiring new techniques of the science and heritage centres and children's museums to bring their own wonderful collections to life, they could capture the popular imagination once again, without ceasing to be museums. If dinosaurs had been able to apply their minds to the subject, they would surely have assumed that their species would survive forever. Museums are dinosaurs today; they now need to evolve into birds.

Spearhead, knapped from bottle glass, North Australian Aborigine, late 19th century.
Museum of Archaeology, Cambridge

CHAPTER FIVE

Looking at Things

Collections can only regain their significance in museums if the actual process of looking can become interesting again. But can it? Today we rarely give anything a second glance. One only has to notice the eyes of someone watching television to see the lack of focus in their stare. It is rather like the difference between the look of an animal in a zoo and the look of an animal in the wild. People in the past looked at each other, and at the world, much more intensely than we tend to do today. The complex and extremely ancient beliefs surrounding the 'evil eye' are but one instance of this. The first covetous glance thrown by someone at the possessions of another was thought to be the most piercing look of all, and many cultures around the globe developed elaborate symbols and procedures to avert its destructive power. Among the peoples of North Africa, for example, the extensive jewellery worn by young brides on their wedding day, and the patchwork jackets worn by soldiers as they rode into battle, both contained within their elaborate patterning, symbolic shapes that were believed to protect their wearers against such envious glances.

Even in the 19th century, people must have looked at things differently from the way we do today. The world was still visually intriguing even to scientists. The question that Darwin tried to answer was: why does nature look the way it does? The word 'species' derives from the Latin *specere,* meaning to look at. Species are, essentially, animals and plants that look alike. Until Darwin, no one really understood why they did. Our glazed looks today do not just stem from the fact that we are now inundated with images; we have also lost much of our sense of wonder at the world. Museums now need to find ways to encourage the visitors who come through their doors to look afresh and questioningly again. One way museums can do this is by bringing what they have sharply into focus. Museums are mainly about learning through looking; they can provide vivid visual experiences that are unlike anything we get from a computer, a book or, most of the time, from everyday life. Not only are visual experiences in museums unimpeded, they are unequivocally three-dimensional. With our bifocal vision, we see three-dimensionally even when we are looking at a work of art as apparently flat as an illuminated manuscript.

The experience of looking at the original Lindisfarne Gospels is much more intense than looking at a modern facsimile version, even if the copy is virtually the same in size and colour. It is a hundred-fold richer experience than seeing a virtual version sunk beneath the hazy surface of a computer screen, even if this enables you to turn its pages, as you now can in a new display at the British Library, and will soon be able to on the island of Lindisfarne where the Gospels were originally used. The reason why the experience of seeing the original Lindisfarne Gospels is much more rewarding than looking at any reproduction is because you sense, by doing so, that you are really in touch with the past. And in a way you are, because seeing is a sense, and a form of touching. Looking at a silky smooth colour reproduction or a glowing computer screen, you cannot help but be aware that these are products of our times. The original Lindisfarne Gospels are painted on vellum made from calfskin, soaked, stretched and then scraped clean. Shadows of spines can be seen running across the pages, because no matter how well the skins were pressed, the form of the animal re-asserts itself. Our eyes detect even the slighter changes in surface texture. No reproduction allows you to appreciate the uneven thickness of paint in these Gospels, as the artist starts with his brush full and then tails off when his brush is empty. What is remarkable, looking at the Lindisfarne Gospels in the original, is that you are immediately aware that it is painted by hand on an animal skin. The world in that age seems to breathe around it. You have the sensation that you are looking over the monk's shoulder watching him paint, as you study this great volume in the British Library. Then all the love, care and infinite patience that went into the creation of this Gospel become palpable. This is an unforgettably evocative experience and one you could never have without seeing the original.

Velasquez's *Las Meninas* in the Prado

Before I actually saw Velasquez's *Las Meninas* of 1656 in the Prado, I had no idea of its scale. In fact the main figures in it are life-size and so lifelike that I felt I was looking not at a picture but through a hole in the wall. It was as though the Infanta, Margarita Teresa, and her aides were just in the next room, breathing and talking. Behind them, in half shadow, stood the painter himself, looking at the canvas and at me – or rather, at the mirror facing him that I had initially read as a hole in the wall. Was I watching the scene through a one-way mirror? Or was I in the room with them, and Velasquez about to add me to the scene? I suddenly had the extraordinary sensation that I was. I had been transported into the painting. This explained its scale. Velasquez's painting had embraced me. The beautiful gentleness of its light, its breadth, its clarity and humanity were, for those memorable moments, the air I breathed. No one could experience this sensation, which I am sure Velasquez intended to create, by looking at a reproduction of this picture in a book. Because we see three-dimensionally, the space in which we view things becomes a vital aspect of our experience when viewing exhibits in a museum, even when they are two dimensional.

No reproduction can prepare one for the sight of the treasures of Tutankhamun in the Museum of Egyptian Antiquities in Cairo. The effect of so much gold, as you walk through the galleries, harnessing the light as if it were molten, is irreproducible. On each side of the four-square golden Canopic Shrine stand four small golden goddesses. They have their backs to the outside world and extend their arms to protect the inner shrine from any evil. But they do not touch it. Moreover, each of them turns her face away, as if they dare not even look upon the shrine before them. I know of few more profound images of tender care. And yet, you can only really experience this if you see the object for yourself, in three dimensions. The extraordinary sensation of tenderness is only expressed by the positioning of these goddesses so close to, yet not touching the Shrine. This emotive use of space cannot be sensed in any reproduction or on any screen.

But how can a museum encourage its visitors to look more intensely at less remarkable, though potentially fascinating things? Partly just by putting them into a museum. The artificiality of the museum space legitimises, for example, the presence of a shark in a tank in a gallery, whatever one thinks of it as a work of art. Over the last decade or so, modern art galleries have come increasingly to look like museums run by curators who have lost their marbles. The very existence of museums depends on their right to lift something out of one context and use it in another. The object itself has not changed; it is just that our view of it has. A roughly carved figure of a naked man, with mother-of-pearl eyes and a head of real human hair, pierced all over with three-inch nails driven deep into the splitting wood becomes, in the museum, an example of African art and not, as it might have been originally, a way of inflicting pain and suffering on those you fear or hate. Both views can be true and need not exclude each other. They can indeed enhance each other's meaning. One can look at things in more ways than one.

Aristotle believed that knowledge itself began with seeing. He looked around him at life as it was, not as he was told it ought to be, or as a shadow of divinity. Crucially, he believed that there is nothing in the intellect which is not first experienced by sensation. The physical experience of the world, above all the visual experience, enables one to understand the material universe. Leonardo spent a lifetime passionately recording in minute detail everything he could see. He believed that eventually he would be able, by this study, to determine the nature of the soul. For John Ruskin, seeing was, if anything, even more essential to our existence. He wrote in his critique of the works of J. M. W. Turner, *Modern Painters,* that 'the greatest thing a human soul ever does in this world is to *see* something, and tell what it *saw* in a plain way … To see clearly is poetry, prophecy and religion, – all in one.' Mostly we take seeing for granted. The idea that we can develop our ability to see would strike a lot of people as odd, but that is exactly what Ruskin believed. We can all admire the skill of someone who has mastered their craft; the eye and hand co-ordination of a glass blower or stone carver can be electrifying. When a fine cricketer has his eye in, he sees the ball coming and knows instantly how to respond to it. This is visual intelligence and it can be very fast. Our medieval cathedrals were designed by the eye as well as by the ruler. They are the creation of visual experience and intelligence. Ruskin drew nearly every day of his life, to help him understand what he saw around him, and to train his eyes, as he put it, to see more clearly. He believed that drawing was the foundation for visual thought, just as writing was the foundation for verbal thought. His writings on drawing were designed not to teach people how to draw, but how to see. They were not manuals for artists, but training for life. He believed that if we looked more closely and with more feeling at the world around us, we would care for it and make it better.

Drawing is the oldest, simplest and still probably the best 'interactive' used in museums. I always take a pocket sketchbook with me when I visit museums because I cannot stop myself wanting to draw something I find interesting to look at. I want to act with my hands while I look and, also, slow down the process of looking, so that I can glean more. Drawing helps me to absorb what I have seen, turn it over in my mind, and remember the sensations I enjoyed while I was looking. It used to be a common sight to see students drawing in museums, and many galleries had formal and even physical links with their local art schools. The Art Institute of Chicago is an art school and a museum. A special door used to link the Royal College of Art and the Victoria & Albert Museum when these institutions were neighbours, so that students could go easily between the two. But recently some museums have even forbidden drawing for insurance reasons, fearing graffiti on the pictures. Drawing in galleries is not just useful for students; it can be an aid to contemplation for people with no particular training or flair for it. The eye and the hand have a correlation that can be developed over time. A key task of the museum today is to develop the visual acuity of its visitors. This is not an easy task, particularly when the material one is using is full of complex meanings that are not immediately apparent.

In 1985, Sheffield Arts Department recreated a small museum, the Ruskin Gallery, which the great Victorian art critic and social commentator had given to the city a century before. Many of the things in it had a broadly symbolic and often deeply personal significance for John Ruskin, but contemporary accounts of visitors' reactions to the museum show the difficulties that the original curator faced in communicating these layers of meanings. When they re-opened the museum, they did their best to bring out the imaginative associations that Ruskin discovered between, say, an opal in its natural setting and a watercolour study of a medieval missal showing an angel's wing, by displaying these alongside each other with quotations by Ruskin. These were not printed but written by the calligrapher, Lida Cardozo Kindersley, with a brush in changing, coloured inks, so that his words became exhibits in themselves and enhanced the visual impact of the whole display. But what was lacking was the means to take visitors into the inner recesses of Ruskin's thinking.

Ruskin had given the museum two of his most beautiful watercolours: a wonderful miniature study of Rose la Touche, the young girl he was in love with, every hair delicately painted and her eyes the palest azure, as well as one of his finest studies of a peacock's breast feather, the downy end of it delicately burning into the deep aquamarine of its main, arching spray. Just by looking at these two exhibits, it would be difficult to comprehend their common purpose. Ruskin drew the peacock's feather to show how it was midway in form between the scale of a fish and the fur of a mammal and to demonstrate how wrong he thought Darwin was to assert that nature had developed visual beauty merely as a vehicle for sexual attraction and selection of the fittest. His portrait of Rose, too, had a similar aim; he passionately believed the love he felt for her was pure, not sexual. But can the subtle thoughts behind such sights ever be conveyed in a museum?

The Women's Museum, Aarhus

One of the challenges for museums today is to create displays that express emotional, not just factual, content. Jette Sandahl, the curator of the Women's Museum in Aarhus in Denmark, put on an exhibition about the night and its role in women's lives; in death, sickness and birth, in lovemaking and dreams. It charted the changes that artificial lighting had made to women's life at work, at play and in the street. One gallery dealt with fear; it was the only one bathed in light. The room was filled with a high-pitched sound that some people experience when coming out of a faint. In the centre, on the floor, was an overturned woman's bike, its front wheel still spinning. Facts were given about how few women venture out at night and what proportion are attacked. In a case along one of the walls were real objects that women carried to defend themselves, such as a bunch of keys with one turned out, as it would have been when clutched in a fist in readiness against an attack. An ordinary object like this, when imaginatively displayed, can acquire a considerable symbolic power. Many might think that this display about the night was more an artistic installation than a museum one, and yet it was very much about history, the history of real experiences and feelings. In Jette Sandahl's work, the artist and the curator meet.

Peter Greenaway, the film-maker, on his own initiative produced a series of large installations in museums in the late 1980s and early 1990s, in which he took objects that interested him from collections and arranged them exactly as he liked, using lighting and theatrical devices to communicate what he felt about them. *Some Organising Principles* was the title of the exhibition that Greenaway put on at the Glynn Vivian Gallery in Swansea. From 17 Welsh museums, he selected over 800 objects that measured, timed, weighed, counted, and numbered the world in different ways. Visitors immediately grasped what the display was about just by looking at the objects, which ranged from a remarkable circular, industrial bottle-washer to a row of plaster heads illustrating variations in physiognomy; from all manner of scales, rulers, callipers and compasses to Dürer's disturbing engraving of *Melancholia* (1514). In this picture, the figure of Melancholia sits huddled and lost in thought, with a pair of dividers in her hand, and suspended above her head a bell, a balance of weights and an hourglass; in the distance, a rainbow arches over the ocean's flat horizon. Using traditional museum showcases and conventional hanging arrangements, Greenaway created a classic and ordered display that was actually more about the perilous closeness of chaos, an evocation of a time when measuring was a step into the unknown.

Greenaway's display in the Louvre was more conventional. He managed to create a sequence of powerful poetic experiences just by putting one image next to another, without any special lighting or effects. His theme was *Le Bruit des Nuages*, which he translated as 'flying out of this world'. Using flight as his theme, Greenaway rapidly took the visitor into many areas of experience. As he wrote in the catalogue: 'In the English language, flight also means escape. In French, to fly is to steal. Fliers are thieves escaping.' The exhibition juxtaposed objects that no museum would normally put together. An image of St Anthony being tortured by devils as he hovers over his desert hermitage was related to a man being tortured by gravity, as he is suspended by a rope and pulley before a tribunal of the Inquisition. Looking at these images while imagining sensations of flight gave one a totally new understanding of pictures that one might have no more than glanced at in a more conventional presentation. Greenaway, by such juxtapositions, revealed the poetry inherent in objects that had never been apparent before.

An imaginative approach to display can introduce emotions not usually found in museums, such as humour. Tim Hunkin, a well-known automata sculptor in Britain, was invited to experiment with a gallery in the Science Museum in London. He called his display *The Secret Life of the Home*. Every exhibit is accompanied by cartoons to show how it was used, a top-hat iron for example; or by simple interactives, such as operating a see-through lavatory, complete with plastic turd. Above the case about refrigeration, hanging face down from the ceiling, is an old fridge. As you walk under it, the door opens and a polar bear's paw reaches out. The device is at once disturbing and funny. Its emotional impact springs from one's awareness of the effect that emissions from refrigeration units are having on the polar bears' natural habitat. In a disused industrial building in Botallach, Cornwall, David Kemp created the Sunset Culture Museum, a totally spoof, but bewilderingly convincing museum (currently closed, pending re-location). He imagined himself to be a 7th-millennium archaeologist who had discovered fragmentary relics of our own, by now, totally forgotten society. He then reconstructed these to show how he believed they were used as cult objects, artefacts and tools, revealing by doing so the gods and goddesses that we worshipped. The votive images in the cases were so compelling and the labels so deadpan, that it was often some time before visitors to the museum recognised the bits of computer keyboards, cars and electrical circuits they comprised, and when they laughed, they did so all the more when they realised the joke was on themselves.

The Museum of Jurassic Technology, Los Angeles

The Museum of Jurassic Technology crouches between a carpet store and a Thai restaurant, in the middle of downtown Los Angeles. It sees itself as a living continuum of the early 'cabinets of curiosities'. Visitors are held in a state of suspension between belief and disbelief, and it is a deeply disorientating experience. One small wall-case contains a luminescent green beetle and a stone, similar in shape and colour. You are invited to press a button beside each and hear a similar high-pitched squeak emitted, apparently, from each exhibit. The label explains the phenomenon of protective auditory mimicry. The beetle when attacked emits the same sound as the pebble is claimed to do when it is at rest – and so the predator, presumably, mistakes it for an inedible, quiescent stone. Another exhibit, a horn grown on the back of a woman's head, purports to come from the collection of the Museum Tradescantium. In another case, a laser projects onto the stuffed head of a wolf a tiny moving image of a man sitting in a chair imitating a wolf howling. This is a portrait of one of the many animal impersonators who work for the film industry. Behind a magnifying lens, a full-length statue of Pope John Paul II in all his regalia stands in the eye of a needle, carved and painted by the Soviet-American émigré, Hagop Sandaldjian, who only worked in the split seconds of calm between each of his heartbeats. The Museum of Jurassic Technology, created by its curator, David Wilson (not to be confused with Sir David Wilson, the recently retired Director of the British Museum), is a celebration of the world of wonder from which museums sprung and that they now need to recreate.

Everything has the potential to become an object of wonder; it just depends on how you look at it. Take a cheap, modern, mass-produced wine glass of the type you can hire for parties and imagine, for a moment, that it is in a museum. There are many ways of looking at this glass. You can look at it from an aesthetic viewpoint and appreciate it artistically, admire its proportions or the gleam of its reflections. You can look at it from a scientific viewpoint to discover how it was manufactured, the physical properties that govern its form, the way it has to be cupped in the hand, in order to warm and swill the wine and release its bouquet. You can look at it from a historical viewpoint, to understand how factors at the time that it was made governed its form and function, the convention of drinking table wine out of a stemmed glass, a vestige in this case, perhaps, of class pretensions. (In France, it is ordinarily swallowed by the tumbler.) Or you can view it from a psychological perspective, and read into its form symbols of our unconscious aspirations, desires and fears. One only has to imagine it displayed next to a jar used for beer for the point to be made.

In large museums, the aesthetic perspective is largely dealt with by the Fine and Decorative Arts Department, the scientific perspective by the Science and Technology Department and the historical by the Department of

History. No one deals with the psychological perspective. One could argue that psychology is an intrinsic part of aesthetics, that it cannot be studied out of a historical context and that it is a science in itself, so it is covered by the other three. If so, then those departments need to think about psychology much more consciously than they do at present, because what they choose to put on show and how they display it will influence the visitor subliminally, if not consciously. Museums operate symbolically whether they like it or not. And much of what they contain is symbolic. This is the view of the world we have lost, that museums have to help to recreate, if they are to give their visitors some understanding of life at a time when it was difficult to believe that death was merely a disintegration and life nothing more than a chemical reaction. A case can be made for doing away with all departments in museums and creating one for symbolism, because all objects become symbolic when they enter a museum, and the job of the curator is to interpret them.

So, let us imagine this commonplace wine glass in a museum. A curator in the Decorative Arts Department could begin his interpretation of it by telling you that it was designed in 1952 as a result of a competition set by the Ravenhead Glass Company for students of the Royal College of Art in London, to produce a classic wine glass that could be easily mass produced, at a low price. He might display it with other cheap glasses of its period to illustrate the effectiveness of its design. His colleague in the Fine Arts Department, looking at the glass purely aesthetically, might lift it out of this context and place it on a pedestal so that its fine proportions could be fully appreciated. It is a classic in the way the Ravenhead Glass Company hoped it would be. Its form and function are completely in harmony. It is an image of balance and equality, of the aesthetic attraction of democracy and egalitarianism, of quality for all; a Greek temple to Bacchus for our times. The curator in the History Department would not be satisfied with this interpretation; he would want to show the glass in its social context, as an artefact with a history, that someone has thought about, designed and made at a specific time, with a specific group of people in mind. He would see in this glass the popularisation of wine-drinking and its challenge to beer, the post-war expansion of the middle classes, and the emergence of a new, unified Europe.

As a visitor, you may think that you are the most active interpreter of this glass when it is in a museum. You bring to the activity of looking at it your memories of the dinners and parties you went to when you drank from glasses like this. If you had not had those experiences, would this glass mean as much to you when you looked at it? Almost certainly not. In this instance, the sight of the glass has triggered a memory, rather than a direct experience.

It is the key to the door rather than the door itself. If your looking at the glass had only led to a memory, then the experience of looking at it would be forgotten. Museums provide many occasions for memories, and there is nothing wrong with that, but it is more rewarding if objects can do more. They can provide memorable experiences in themselves. But how can looking at this glass in itself become a door to a new experience?

An easy way for the historian to expand the meaning of this glass, would be to place a medieval glass beside it; one also used for everyday drinking. Looking at them together would speak volumes about what has happened to the world since the Middle Ages. The imperfect, handmade, medieval glass, with its rich colour and individual character, evokes a totally different world from that connected with the mechanical lines of the plain and utterly functional modern wine glass beside it. Just looking at these two objects could give us a profound understanding of the way we have changed our world. Two such glasses could encapsulate, for us, the difference between the pre- and the post-industrial age. And if our imagination is so stimulated that we begin to build a picture of the life that was led around the old glass, in a world where everything was made by hand, then we would be able to imagine how unbelievably strange this glass of ours would have appeared to someone of those times. It is then not the old glass that comes to look odd, but our own.

The science curator, too, could use this glass in a purely visual way. If he was trying to show what is meant by the centre of gravity, just by eye, without demonstrating it practically, then what better way could he chose than to use this glass? Its stem is an expression not just of the ever-present downward pull of gravity, but of the force that is needed to resist it, beautifully expressed in a transparent form. The scientist could also use the glass to explore chemical change. Imagine a display with this glass standing on a bed of sand, so that we can appreciate the raw material from which glass is made and how that material is changed in the process. And then imagine this glass on a bed of sand put beside another display which shows a piece of coal next to the diamond into which it can be transformed, under colossal pressure. And then, let us say, you added to these two images of change a bar of lead next to a nugget of gold, then we could, perhaps, begin to understand how so many scientists believed for many centuries that, surely, there had to be a way in which one could change base metal into gold. As recently as 1695, Frederick Duke of Hesse-Hamburg presented to King Christian V of Denmark a piece of alchemical gold that he swore he had made himself out of lead, together with two samples of the lead he had used. We are entering what would now be thought of as symbolic territory, though it was considered to be scientific once. But this is just the beginning of the symbolism that this glass can convey. If we were, for example, to put next to these displays on the transformation of sand into glass, coal into diamond and lead into gold, two more glasses, one with water in it and another one with wine, we might get a glimpse of how exceptional and generous a symbol the miracle at Cana was, which reversed this process of clarification. Or you could place next to a glass of wine, a glass of brandy from which it could have been distilled; not water transformed into wine, but wine into a different kind of water – *aqua vitae* – or as it is in Gaelic, *usquebaugh*, which we now call whisky, the water of life; itself a process of purification, the manifestation of a spirit, though admittedly of a more mundane kind.

It is the museum's job to make its collections meaningful today. Objects from the distant past are often immediately interesting, simply because they are out of place. Museums get away with putting old things on display because they are curiosities. John Tradescant the Elder, when establishing his collection that later became the Ashmolean Museum in Oxford, wrote to the Secretary of the Navy in 1625, asking him to tell all merchants of his interest in acquiring 'Any thing that Is Strange'. The most historically evocative glass objects I have ever seen are the exquisitely knapped spear and arrow heads, made in the late 19th and early 20th century from pieces of bottle glass and, sometimes, toughened glass taken from the insulators on telegraph poles, by the Aboriginal people of the Northern Territories – a crystalline fusion of the Stone Age with our own telecommunications age. A fine group of these are to be found in the Australian Museum in Sydney. In the Pitt Rivers Museum in Oxford, there is a prehistoric flint arrowhead set in a silver mount. It was collected in Italy in 1901, at which time it was thought to be a thunderbolt. But interest even in such evocative things as these can quickly fade if their wider significance is not revealed. Museums need to provide more than curiosities.

A wine glass in a museum is automatically different from a wine glass in life. For a start, if this glass were in a museum, it would almost certainly not contain any wine. Glasses in museums never have anything in them because objects in museums are lifted out of use. This is at once a limitation and an advantage for a museum, because it means that though the objects they possess are useless, their meaning is no longer limited to their use. Museums usually acquire objects when they cease to be useful, like old cars, mangles or even paintings. This link between museum acquisition and the end of normative life is illustrated today by the demand by native peoples for the return of artefacts. They want to revive lost traditions and put back into use the ceremonial and religious objects that have survived, until now, as 'useless' objects in museums. An instance of this that gets wide sympathy in the West is the call, since the fall of Communism, for the return of Christian treasures to churches in Russia. Many icons that were in museums are now being kissed by worshippers again, a practice that would not have been allowed if they had remained in museums!

So, if most of what we have in museums has ceased to be useful, what is the use of it? A glass that you cannot drink from – what is the purpose of that? When an object is in a museum, we need to not just recall its original function, but to use it to muse. Museum professionals often overlook the poetry of objects that is there for them to discover. In the Gallery of Modern Art in Glasgow, wine glasses are included in a display created by an artist, although he does not describe himself as such, though he is one of the few to have genuinely continued, not imitated, the work of Joseph Cornell. He considers himself just a communicator, which is a good enough definition of an artist for me. His name is Aidan Shingler, and he suffers from schizophrenia. Over a ten-year period he created a sequence of exhibits of objects, through which he tried to express what it was like to be schizophrenic. He packed a suitcase, for example, with all the things he thought he would need when aliens came to collect him, as he believed they would. The suitcase included a large torch (to guide them down from the sky), his passport, a toothbrush with some Signal toothpaste, and some food for the journey, including sweets such as Milky Ways, Mars Bars and Galaxies which he believed had been named for this purpose. In the displays, he put a circle of wine glasses, each filled with water, around the circumference of a map of the moon's surface. He wrote on the label accompanying this exhibit: 'I believed that the moon was directly controlling my mind. The thinking behind this belief was as follows: the moon affects the oceans, the sea is of course water, and human beings are composed of 80 per cent water. Therefore, my deduction was that the moon affects mind and body. During this phase I drank enormous quantities of H_2O.' So the glasses have become a vehicle through which we can gain an understanding of a state of mind. This understanding is expressed symbolically in a variety of ways: by the clarity of these two materials, glass and water; by the crescent-shaped reflected lights; and by the bowl of the glass, like the moon itself, the earth with its oceans, or the dome of a head with thoughts contained within it. And when one adds to that one's awareness of the pressing, urgent thoughts in Shingler's mind, compared with the potential stillness of untroubled thoughts, then one can get a glimpse of someone else's life that perhaps one will not forget, and all by looking at an ordinary wine glass.

Many curators might have been reluctant to let me use the glass in this way had it not been ordinary but been instead a rare Venetian specimen. Just because such a glass would have been acquired to show the mastery and beauty of Venetian glass blowing, it does not mean that all other ways of looking at it have to be outlawed. Despite the increasing interest in social history and its impact on art, many art curators today would still be reluctant to let such a glass be used to illustrate class divisions in the 18th century, except perhaps for the briefest period in a temporary exhibition. A science curator would go down on his knees in vain if he were to propose using it to illustrate gravity, even though its incredibly slender stem would make it a most fitting exemplar of this force. He would be quite likely to be refused the use, even if the glass were in store.

Objects today enter museums to become symbolic. This process of transformation is analogous to our efforts to understand the ancient world. In order to do that, we have to enter a world of poetry. Of course, most moments of life then were as mundane as they are today. Yet many of the images that have come down to us from pre-Enlightenment cultures encapsulate moments that were clearly believed to be numinous. Museums offer the potential for everything that enters them to become illuminating and poetic. W.H. Auden defined poetry as 'memorable speech'. It is liberating to think of museums as providing memorable sights.

Armillary sphere, showing how heavenly bodies were believed to rotate around the earth,
made by Antonio Santucci, 1588–1593 CE.
Museum of the History of Science, Florence

CHAPTER SIX

Elitism and Populism

A museum that wants to spread enlightenment has to begin by encouraging visitors to look at its collections. But its task is not over when it has achieved that. The museum then has to ask itself whether as many people as possible are getting as much as they could from this experience. Thousands might queue to see Royal wedding presents or the latest moving dinosaurs, but the challenge facing museums is to give their public something deeply rewarding. Their task is to become popular and profound.

Curators wanting to interpret their collections to a wider audience are in danger of being denigrated as populists. There is often an assumption that if something is popular it must be superficial; but one does not popularise Shakespeare, one promotes him because his work is popular. This is different from being a populist, who would argue that the public's range of interests is narrow and that museums should try to discover and serve only those interests. There is a constant battle to wage against the kind of received opinion which characterises large chunks of culture as obscure or difficult, despite the fact that both children and grown-ups encountering poetry, classical music or paintings and antiquities for the first time, are often fascinated and delighted. The introduction of surtitles, so long resisted by opera aficionados, has led many to this art form. How something is presented can be just as important as what is presented.

Populists deny the appetite that the public has for museums. This does not mean, however, that a scholar working as a curator can bury himself in his subject and expect his public to follow. Curators need to become better acquainted with those who live within reach of their museums, and need to pay attention to wider social and philosophical trends. This is not in order to target some few topics that are guaranteed to bring in huge numbers, but to exploit connections between current public preoccupations and the museum's collections and subject matter. Their consultations should not narrow the list of what can be put on display so that the local Asian community is offered only the museum's temple rubbings, or the local burghers' wives only the museum's Fabergé boxes. There is a difference between getting to know your public and being confined by the knowledge of the least informed. Finding out what the public wants and giving it to them includes allowing them to find out more for themselves. It does not mean giving them what we thought they would find out. It is so easy to lower people's horizons, especially if you

79

are in the powerful position of being the person configuring the landscape. Museum curators are in such a position when they decide their programme of displays, exhibitions and acquisitions. The way to halt dumbing down is for the providers to ask themselves if they are interested in what they are presenting and whether it extends their horizons and increases their understanding of the world. Or are they belittling their potential users, denying the breadth and seriousness of their audiences in order to cynically generate commerce? To guard against that means treating the visitors as equals.

Currently, curators tend to think of collections in terms of their own interests, not those of their visitors. Though the hegemony of curators is being eroded as far as running whole museums is concerned, they are still effectively mini-directors in their own subject areas. It is not so long ago in the larger museums that broken pots went to Archaeology while whole ones went to Decorative Arts, an arrangement as inconvenient as it is arbitrary, and totally bewildering to any visitor. Though collecting areas are becoming more intelligently designated, collections are still ring-fenced, and this has a direct effect on the museum's public. Traditionally, curators are allocated spaces – a more accurate word would be territories – in which to display their collections within a museum. Any encroachment can be taken personally. I know of one curator who never spoke to a colleague again because he hung a boat in the light-well over her space. He claimed that the boat could be seen from his balconies and was therefore part of his display, while she felt her display was being invaded by his oppressive hulk. Curators commonly fill every corner of their jealously guarded terrain, whatever the real needs of the story they want to tell, for fear that the part they do not use might be taken from them. This accounts for the patchwork of different displays one comes across in large, encyclopaedic museums. These can create startling and entertaining contrasts of mood and subject matter, if one is prepared enough not to be bewildered. It can be amusing to try to spot the territorial divisions, and guess the different personalities that govern each space, as one passes from Islam through Invertebrates to the Industrial Revolution.

This is why, in recent years, many museums have imposed a uniform house style that masks the factions still seething underneath. The British Museum was a leader in this approach and inaugurated the reign of the Design Department that has for many years held sway over all its galleries, from the labelling to the actual choice of exhibits. If a curator wants too many objects, these are ruthlessly pruned. Only so many can be displayed on a shelf, with the prerequisite amount of space around each. Every glass, every bowl, every knife, every fork has to be laid out separately. It is always before the feast, never after. A curator would not be allowed to exhibit a collection of antique necklaces spilling out of a jewellery box, as if on someone's dressing-table. Each necklace has to be pinned up separately and the jewellery box exhibited with its lid shut. Many visitors, as a result, miss the point that what are now rarities were once commonplace, much like jewellery in use today.

The policy is still being pursued by the British Museum as it starts to reorganise all of its displays, now that its central circulation has been so beautifully rationalised by the Great Court. The first new gallery to be opened was one dedicated to its African collection, arguably the finest in the world. Superficially the display looks most attractive. The galleries are light and every item is clearly displayed and lit, in gleaming glass showcases, as it would be in an up-market boutique. But, immediately one tries to come to terms with the meaning of each exhibit, the impression of clarity falls apart. For a start, why Africa? It is such a vast and complex continent, with Islam ruling the north, Christianity the south and more ancient tribal cultures dominating the centre and spread throughout, that many doubt if the collective term 'African' has, or has ever had, any real meaning, apart from denoting the world's second largest land mass. It is totally misleading to put Islamic, Christian and tribal artefacts together in one case, as happens again and again in this display, as if they had a common, overarching African identity. This is especially the case if visitors have never been told what these religions are in the first place. It would not be so bad if visitors were at least given a historical perspective on what they are looking at, but they are not given even that. Exhibits are jumbled together regardless of date, as if the cultures of Africa are somehow outside time. That in itself diminishes our appreciation of their achievements. The San culture of southern Africa (one of the most ancient in the world) has provided scholars with a recent breakthrough in the interpretation of the prehistoric cave paintings of France and Spain. The great art of Benin did not spring out of nowhere, nor did it owe its origin to the influence of European art, as was long believed: it grew out of an indigenous tradition that had been developing for well over a millennium. The Ancient Egyptian civilisation could legitimately be termed 'African'. Not to include it here, even in a token way, just because another department in the Museum deals with it (as the curators argue), diminishes further our sense of the cultures of this great continent.

So, if the exhibits are not grouped culturally or chronologically, how are they arranged? Extraordinarily, the British Museum has decided to resort to the outmoded method of displaying exhibits according to how they are made. The new galleries are divided into woodcarving, textiles, brass-casting, pottery and forging. Only a display on 'masquerading' and another on personal adornment attempt to put meaning before matter. The overall effect is of an old-fashioned museum store where all the knives are on one shelf and all the pots on another, regardless of what each object means. So a crude ritual vessel inscribed with female pudenda, which a Bura man once kept next to his head while he slept, made offerings to for good fortune, drank from with only his closest male friend, and which was buried with him when he died, sits next to a wheel-turned, slip-decorated floral flask made in Egypt in the 19th century that would have graced any respectable Victorian mantelpiece, just because they both happen to be made of clay. Visitors would glean much more from these exhibits if they had been grouped together according to their meaning, not the materials from which they were made or their method of manufacture.

Clarity in museums can be deceptive. A row of silver objects shining in a case may look clear and well ordered, and please the eye superficially, but it may not engage the mind or the feelings. Cutlers traditionally displayed their knives on boards, fanned out in attractive patterns to show off their range and skill. A museum could adopt a similar display if it wanted to help its visitors identify a particular maker's products, or date a style or technique, and many do. But if it wanted to put these knives in the context in which they were used, it would have to take a different approach. A knife for an ambassadorial banquet would then not sit so innocently next to one used for killing people in a colonial war. Displays of masks are popular in museums. This seems reasonable enough, until you discover, in one case, a mask used for bawdy entertainment sitting cheek by jowl with one worn at a wake. It is like asking a priest to give you a blessing while a clown tries to make you laugh.

We are now so accustomed to mass-produced consumables and their built-in obsolescence that it can be difficult for us to appreciate how richly associated with meaning possessions were in the past. Everyday utensils were prized and made to last; they were rarely merely functional. If you were poor, a plate or a knife would become identified with you, through use. If you had wealth, such items had to convey messages about status as well as taste. A walk though any period display showing European domestic life from the 16th to the 18th centuries, demonstrates how richly goods and chattel were charged with meaning. In the 16th century, everything from armchairs to cutlery in affluent households was emblazoned with the arms of the owners and declarations of religious allegiances. By the 18th century, heritage is still important, but expressions of piety have been almost entirely replaced by images of happy peasants making hay in the summertime. Their owner's fear of retribution from God has been replaced with fear of retribution from the less well off, fully justified as history showed.

There is some evidence to suggest that the people who lived beside the peat bogs of Denmark 3,000 years ago realised their preservative qualities, as the Ancient Egyptians realised those of the dry desert air, to give the items and bodies they placed there eternal life. The Danes sacrificed extraordinary treasures to the bogs, such as great bronze urns, magnificent curved trumpet-like instruments that can still be played, and the arms and armour, including the horses, of defeated armies. Such things must have cost a great deal to make and acquire, plunder or seize, but their sacrificial value was greater. Several early burials have been preserved in remarkable condition due to the putrefying attributes of the Danish soil. The deceased were laid to rest in their best clothes and jewellery, and they took their most treasured possessions with them into the next world. In the oak coffin of a 30-year-old woman, a bronze cauldron was found containing the remains of a fermented drink brewed from barley and local berries, together with a fine bronze ladle for serving it. In her hand had been placed the matching bronze strainer that went with it. This must have had a special significance for her but its meaning today has been lost. It is perhaps easier to guess why, in an earlier grave, a child was found buried with three crab apples and a toy arrow.

In the elegance of many modern museum displays, personal significance is often cleared away. People themselves are cleared away. How often have I heard curators remark, at the opening of a new display, 'you should see it with no one in it!' A well-known cartoon shows, in one panel, a 'private view' at an exhibition packed with people drinking and talking, though with no one looking at the pictures; while next to it is an image of the 'public view' of the gallery, with no one in it. Once, when I was arguing for money to replace some faded and stained damask wall-lining in a gallery in Glasgow, one of my committee members commented that he thought people went to look at the pictures, not the walls. He had a point: visitors to museums and galleries are far less preoccupied than curators and designers with the overall appearance of their displays. They tend to concentrate on the contents. It is important to leave enough room around an object for it to be fully appreciated, but curators can get rather precious and over-zealous about this, and instead of making the object on show more easily understood, they can easily make it appear more exclusive. The result is that many first-time visitors to museums, particularly those dealing with art, find the atmosphere intimidating. One teenager put it very well: she said of an art gallery which she had visited in a school party, that she did not like the place because she felt everything was looking at her. It is from such experiences that a museum's reputation for elitism grows, even if this might be the opposite of the curator's intention.

Philippe de Montebello at the Metropolitan Museum of Art

Philippe de Montebello, who has been the Director for over 20 years of New York's Metropolitan Museum of Art, does not accept that elitism automatically leads to exclusivity. He is fond of telling the story of an Afro-American pupil who was attending a weekend programme the museum runs for city schoolchildren, and asked him what the museum was doing to combat elitism. De Montebello replied, 'But you're an elitist yourself! This is Saturday, and you're not hanging out on some street corner, are you? You've come here because you want to learn something, or to better yourself in some way, and I'd say that makes you an elitist.' The other kids, he said, applauded. De Montebello thinks elitism is not only compatible with, but is the very essence of democracy; it seeks to bring as many people as possible to a higher level of understanding and appreciation. When asked, 'aren't you an elitist institution?', his answer is, 'that's exactly what we are. That's what art is, and that's what every visitor to the Met is. By crossing the threshold they are joining the elite.' There is an admirable clarity about this. It is perhaps one reason why the museum has been so successful in attracting endowments.

The Metropolitan Museum is absolutely confident about the quality of everything that is within it. What it has, it states, is unquestionably good for you to acquire knowledge about and, if you can afford it, to acquire. It stands like a vast national bank, validating cultural education and cultural acquisition. But generating understanding is based not on telling people what to think, but on inviting them to think for themselves. The Met does not raise possibilities; it gives a set of answers. It might have been more productive to ask the Afro-American pupil why he thought the museum was elitist. Philippe de Montebello's belief is that that perception was false, but whether it is false or not, this young student and presumably many others share this view. Surely it is in the interests of the museum to counteract this perception, and it can only do so if it entertains alternative views.

In 1996, Glasgow Museums organised a large exhibition on the work of Charles Rennie Mackintosh, the *fin-de-siècle* Glasgow architect and designer. The Metropolitan Museum in New York borrowed the exhibition but, when they showed it, they excluded virtually all work by and reference to Margaret Mackintosh, his wife, despite the fact that he worked very closely

with her; they designed interiors and decorations together, and some drawings are signed with both their initials. The curator at the Met did not regard
the work of Margaret to be as good as that of Mackintosh himself, though in
many cases their work was inseparable, and Mackintosh himself certainly regarded it as such. The Met exhibition also neglected the evidence that
Mackintosh and his wife both explored the ideas of Rosicrucianism, which
was widely influential across Europe at that time, especially in artistic circles.
The symbols of the Rose and the Cross have many correspondences in the
work of both Charles Rennie and Margaret Mackintosh. The Met was only
concerned with the aesthetics of formalism. Mackintosh, perhaps in contrast
with other men of his generation, saw his wife as his equal; he was also interested in the relationship between sexuality and creativity. An exploration of
these facts might have attracted a more varied audience to the exhibition.
What the public got instead at the Met was a display, on grey marble, of collectable artefacts by an exceptionally inventive interior designer, not the life's
work of a passionate, intemperate, intensely questioning and creative husband and wife team. The objects were authentic, but the complexity of their
meaning had been reduced to form, colour and line. The Met is elitist not
because it intends to exclude anyone, but because it does so by excluding alternative points of view.

Art galleries everywhere, from the National Gallery in London to the National Gallery of Victoria, are traditionally arranged in a chronological sequence, according to art historical definitions of schools of painting. And,
traditionally, they *are* paintings. There are historical reasons why this category
of art has been given such prominence, over and above its intrinsic popularity and the wealth that has been invested in it. When London's National Gallery was formed, it was debated whether or not it should include sculpture as
well as painting. At the same time, the future arrangement of the Uffizi Gallery was under consideration. It is no coincidence that, during the 1830s and
1840s, when it was decided that the National Gallery should be devoted to
painting, and that all the sculptures in the Uffizi should be moved to the
newly formed National Museum of the Bargello (previously the headquarters of the secret police), the techniques of photography were being developed. Perhaps people recognised that the art of painting was going to need
preserving, though the official reason given was that painting and sculpture
required different ways of seeing, a view that would strike many as somewhat
refined today, and simply incomprehensible to those from earlier times who
were accustomed to seeing sculpture painted.

The sequential arrangement of pictures in galleries, though not as clearly
marked as it would have been even 20 years ago, still embodies the concept

of continuing excellence. The visitor is presented with the peaks of achievement of the Italian Renaissance in one room and Northern Renaissance
painting in another room, even though there were many stimulating cross-
currents between the two. Rubens is often hung near Rembrandt because
they were contemporaries and lived in close proximity, even though the
great schism in Europe between the Catholics and the Protestants ran like a
rift valley between their work. But the majority of visitors to art galleries are
more interested in art than these art-historical divisions. They may never get
around to understanding the chronological development of style, but this
does not invalidate their presence in the gallery or necessarily diminish their
appreciation of the pictures. You do not have to be a musicologist to appreciate Beethoven. Concert-goers would quickly turn away if they were only
given programmes of one school of music at a time, chronologically arranged. Yet that is exactly the diet that art galleries give their audiences.

It would be quite legitimate for an art gallery to put on a display about,
say, the language of painting, to help its visitors appreciate the potential and
scope of this wonderful medium, or to hang a gallery with works of art according to their mood and meaning. A room full of images that profoundly
expressed Christian belief could not only provide a very moving aesthetic
experience, but also help people not of that faith to understand its meaning.
The same treatment could be afforded to Buddhist, Hindu or Muslim art.
For the vast majority of people in the past, and many today, these paintings
and sculptures mean more as religious images than they do as works of art.
There is no reason why art galleries should not cater for their needs. And,
besides religion, there are common human themes that art again and again
comes back to, such as the praise of beauty, man and nature, the fear of death
and dreams of immortality, that are the undercurrents of so much imagery
from Europe though to China. All these are themes that art galleries can
present, alongside more conventional art historical displays, for those who
are interested in such approaches.

Attitudes are beginning to change. Philippe de Montebello at the Met, in
a recent interview, commented that it used to be taken for granted that the
collections were important, but this is no longer the case. Museums cannot
go on assuming that what they say is good *is* good, and they can certainly no
longer expect that visitors will automatically accept their point of view. This
is exactly the case put by the curators of Tate Modern in London to justify
their installation of the modern international collections, which are now
grouped by theme, such as 'nude, action, body' or 'history, memory, society'.
Rather like the pigs in *Animal Farm,* they might be accused of maintaining
that although there is no longer only one view of art, the only valid one is

theirs. It is true that the view that modern art is progressing towards perfect expression, which was promoted by some Western museums of modern art until the 1990s, no longer holds sway. But that does not mean that history itself is invalid. The job of Tate Modern is to sort out the significant art of our times, and no one can do that without a grasp of history. Though currents of creativity are often complex and intertwined, sequences do emerge and times do change. Without history we are adrift on a sea of personal preferences, in a barge of the curator's choosing, at the mercy of his or her predilections, with no overall sense of direction or constellations to steer by. Up to a point, that is quite exciting. But this is the role of a temporary exhibition programme, not a museum's permanent collection. The Rijksmuseum in Amsterdam has recently gone in the opposite direction from the Tate: it has re-hung several of its galleries to tell the history of the Netherlands, because the museum thinks this is not being taught adequately in schools and without history, it maintains, no visitor can really grasp the meaning of the art in its collections.

Officially the Tate now wishes to be called just 'Tate', but I have continued to use the definite article for a number of reasons. This book is about the future of museums and galleries and compares their different achievements to date. The Tate cannot drop the definite article on the grounds that it is unique, like London, or Disneyland (which, though replicated, is exactly so), or heaven (which, though they are several, are each believed to be exclusive). The Tate is just another gallery of modern and national art. Nor can the Tate justify dropping its definite article on the grounds that it has become a brand. There is now Tate Modern and Tate Britain, not to mention Tate Liverpool and Tate St Ives, and, who knows, the Tate might have aspirations to spawn other galleries, like the Guggenheim has in Bilbao. But there still remains an umbrella organisation called the Tate, which has a real existence and is not just a label. It is not often appreciated that the Tate is so structured at present that its galleries are only exhibition venues. Tate Modern and Tate Britain do not have their own collections, nor do they collect. Their directors are in charge of the displays but there is a separate director who is in charge of the collections, though he has no gallery in which to show them, only a store; and over all these directors presides a super-director, who actually collects. The Tate, as a collection and as a collecting organisation, does exist separately from its public galleries. It cannot pretend to elevate itself above comparison. So, for the purposes of this book, the Tate remains *the* Tate.

Museums need to state clearly the criteria they use to build their collections, to give their public the chance to judge their achievements and to encourage debate about what they collect. The National Gallery in London now makes room for contrasting aesthetic responses to art, though they have not gone so far as to invite their visitors to comment on which works of art they think the gallery should purchase, something Tate Modern could also certainly do. They have, however, instituted a series of public debates in which two speakers argue for and against a painting, after which the audience votes. It is impossible to imagine such open candour in Victorian times, when the gallery was founded. Museums, then, were authoritarian. Visitors to museums today expect to see authentic things, but they cannot be guaranteed to accept the museum's view of them.

Today, many art galleries in Britain display visitors' comments about the works on show, some for and some against. People come to see how the debate is ranging and whether or not anyone has responded to their remarks. The National Museum and Gallery of Wales has photocopied children's remarks and put them next to the paintings alongside the conventional labels. When I was there, all the visitors seemed to be reading the children's comments, many of them moving and revealing, some trenchant and funny, rather than reading the official information. The children's remarks often made one question one's own response and stimulated one to look back at the works a second time, whereas the curatorial labels tended to close off the experience; when they had finished reading them many visitors turned away. Labelling, which often serves the museum administration rather than the visitor, is an obvious obstacle to visitor confidence and enjoyment. Curators at conferences talk forever about labels; whole manuals have been written about how they should be compiled, but the only criterion for judging the effectiveness of a label is whether it leads the reader to look at the object again with greater understanding.

Curators who spend their lives with their collections naturally think, since they do not need any help interpreting what they see, that it is rather condescending to others to provide them with that help. So they restrict themselves to providing facts, and rarely try to convey the excitement they feel, even though it is precisely their enthusiasm that could really start the visitor on his or her journey of discovery. What would people think if, say, they came across the *Mona Lisa* unprepared and unawares? Would they know how to begin to read the enigma of her expression, and would they appreciate its remarkable technical achievement if they were accustomed, as virtually everyone is today, to colour photography and moving pictures? And what would they think of this lady in a low-cut dress, if they were Muslim or Chinese? Even such a universal work of art as the *Mona Lisa* needs interpretation for its significance to be fully grasped. The *Mona Lisa* was the product of a journey that had taken Leonardo several decades, as he searched for a way to depict the soul. It is possible to imagine an entire museum that would take you through the Ren-aissance and through the study of Leonardo's mind, finally leading you to this one great painting. Creating such a journey is the art of the museum, but as it is the visitors to the Louvre file pass the *Mona Lisa*, most of them only wanting to be photographed in front of it, at best wondering what all the fuss is about. A work as famous as the *Mona Lisa* merits interpretation, if only because it is so famous. Understanding, like creativity, is the result of a jour-ney. Picasso said, famously, 'I don't seek, I find'. Though later in his life he wondered if he had not meant to say this the other way around, his discover-ies even if they remained elusive, were the result of searching. Museums take one on journeys that lead to discoveries. Picasso never painted a totally ab-stract painting because, he said, he wanted to provide a figurative stepping-stone into the picture – a recognisable way in for anyone, whether or not they knew anything about art. Museums need to be equally generous if they want to appeal to the people who do not go to them at present.

Nottingham Castle Museum and Art Gallery once made a time-lapse videotape of visitor behaviour in a gallery. Visitors came in at the door, looked about, and almost all of them turned immediately to the left (as the majority of people instinctively do, oddly enough, when entering a gallery). Each visitor then began to walk along the wall of the gallery, looking steadi-ly at each picture in turn. The remarkable thing about this video was that it showed how almost every visitor turned away from the display at about the same point, even though there was no natural break in the display there. They had all become bored at the same moment. After turning away from the wall, the visitors usually wandered into the centre of the gallery, like de-magnetised iron filings, glanced around the whole gallery and then left. Mu-seum curators tend to think of the spaces they have to fill before thinking about holding their visitors' interest.

The way to tackle space-filling at its roots is by doing away with perma-nently assigned exhibition spaces and making the whole museum subject to a regular review of visitors' needs. On commonly owned ground, one can encourage creative diversity. Museums need to become less like textbooks and more like magazines that contain articles of varying length according to the subject and its potential to interest its readers. Curators are fearful that their displays will become superficial if they adopt this approach and the re-sult will be a sound-bite museum. But that is why the concentration on the objects as a starting point is so important. It allows the museum to tell a short story with one object or a long one with a whole series of objects. Poetry can be as condensed as a haiku or as extended as a saga; it can be lyrical or political, dramatic or comic, erotic or satiric, a popular ballad or a metaphysical sonnet. Such a range of displays will be no more superficial to the visitor than an anthology of poetry, a sequence of varied and profound experiences, which can be valued individually or cumulatively. What is crucial about this approach is that the curator begins with an object from the collection and the effect it can have on the visitor, not with a curatorial category to illustrate or a space to fill. As John Ruskin wrote in 1879, 'You can more see 20 things worth seeing in an hour than you can read 20 books worth reading in a day'.

Galileo's Finger

Just around the back of the Uffizi Gallery, overlooking the River Arno, stands Florence's Museum of the History of Science. It contains many remarkable exhibits, including an array of 18th-century waxworks lovingly made to illustrate the development of the foetus in the womb and the problems of childbirth and, in another room, the middle finger of Galileo's right hand, inexplicably embalmed. But by far the most important object is the great scientist's modest telescope, through which he observed, for the first time in human history, the moons of Jupiter. A couple of galleries away there is a remarkable armillary sphere, a working model of the heavens, constructed only a couple of decades before Galileo made his discoveries. It stands 12 feet high, and its girth is nearly as great. Through a bewilderingly complex latticework of overlapping golden rings, one can just make out our dark planet sitting solidly in the centre. It would seem even more fixed if the cranking system could still be operated and all the golden rings revolved.

Galileo's telescope is tucked away in the corner of a room full of telescopes, in a display about the history of this instrument. The armillary sphere is the centrepiece of a gallery devoted to a collection of heavenly spheres and terrestrial globes. The museum only attracts a handful of visitors, but few among them notice the significance of what they are looking at, let alone of their conjunction. Were Galileo's simple little telescope to be placed next to the colossal contraption of the armillary sphere, his revolutionary idea could have been beautifully encapsulated. So, too, could the power of thought. The complexity of the armillary sphere was the result of centuries of painstaking observations, calculations and formulations, and what it demonstrates is observably true to someone standing on the earth. But all this weight of thought was wrong, as Galileo's observation proved. Precisely how wrong could be demonstrated most clearly if an astrolabe were exhibited on the other side of Galileo's telescope, showing how we now understand the motion of the planets, moons and stars – as being much more open and arguably more beautiful, with us moving, too. Such a display would not just show the power of new ideas, but the power that is invested in traditional ideas. The heavenly host that circle the earth in the armillary sphere are all gilded. The arms of the Medici emblazon its outer reaches and on top is a golden cross, demonstrating clearly who then owned the heavens, and our thoughts about them. How moving and telling it would then be to read Galileo's 'Renunciation of his Suspicions', and see the instruments of torture he only had to be shown to make him sign.

The museum had Galileo's telescope restored in 1996, but only shows it in a case in the corner. It would be perfectly possible to construct a display so that visitors could look through, but not touch, Galileo's telescope, even if they could only see at the end of it a mirrored projection of Jupiter's moons. Many of the visitors who queue around the corner for the Uffizi might be attracted by such an experience, even if only to tell their friends, 'I looked down Galileo's telescope!' A Zen Buddhist monk once pointed to the moon, and told his students off for looking at his finger. The Museum of the History of Science has Galileo's finger. But why promote that to the world when they could promote his thoughts?

The fate of the iceman, Ötzi, illustrates perfectly how museums manage to restrict public interest in what they have by the manner in which they present it, even when they add a world–class attraction to their collection. The discovery of Ötzi in 1991 was in archaeological terms as important as the unearthing of Tutankhamun's tomb at the beginning of the 20th century. He was the earliest human being to be found, wearing his everyday clothes and carrying his everyday belongings. After a protracted fight for possession (he was found within yards of the Italian–Austrian border), he was allocated to the curators in Bolzano, a small town in the Italian Alps. Instead of building a new museum for him alone, they seized on the opportunity to create a new museum for all their collections. So, visitors who have come round the world to see Ötzi in the South Tyrol Museum of Archaeology are first faced with a case, one of the longest I have seen in any museum, containing row upon row of tiny flints demonstrating differences between Mesolithic and Neolithic culture. No explanation is given as to how these relate to Ötzi. Most visitors I observed were, by now, already either confused or bored. Few would realise, and it took me some time to do so, that they were embarking on a story not about Ötzi, but about the archaeology of the Southern Tyrol.

Ötzi's story begins on the first floor. Here, through a window, one can see Ötzi's body lying on a metal trolley, as in an operating theatre. The extraordinary possessions that were found with him, such as the beautiful birch-bark basket that contained, wrapped in maple leaves, chips of charcoal – originally glowing embers used for making fire – were laid out in sterile rows in long, low, grey cases, so darkly lit they were almost impossible to see. At least there was a reconstruction of Ötzi himself, standing, wrapped in his fine furs and grass cloak, grasping an axe in his left hand (though the weals on that wrist suggest he held something more painful), his right foot raised on a boulder, his mouth slightly open as if he was about to call out, and his eyes staring boldly ahead. It is difficult to relate this heroic figure to the strained, lean corpse one had just seen.

Ötzi merits a whole museum to himself. One floor alone could be devoted to fire, another to the contents of his stomach, and another to his remarkable axe. So much is known about the terrain around his body – they even found a fingernail that had been carried some distance by the ice (which showed, incidentally, that Ötzi had suffered a traumatic experience a few months before he died), that it would be possible to reconstruct the mountainside exactly as it would have looked at the time of his death, with Ötzi sitting on the ledge where he died, not standing in a heroic pose, as in an illustration for an old-fashioned boys' comic or a still from a bad film. Visitors could then interpret the evidence for themselves, and wonder why, for example, he had placed his quiver with its two arrows ready for shooting and twelve unfinished shafts on a stone slab five yards away, or why his bearskin cap was lying on the ledge beside him, as if it had rolled off his head as he lay down to sleep, or whether he had placed it there, because its straps were untied. Visitors could then, perhaps, begin to experience what it could have been like to look at the world through Ötzi's eyes, and wonder what might have been in his thoughts as his eyes closed for the last time.

Ötzi has been effectively reburied in this museum in Bolzano, not just because of the context in which he is being shown, but because of the light levels at which he and his possessions can be seen. Many objects in museums are, today, barely visible. For those with impaired sight, museums have become a virtual no-go area, and that includes many elderly people – in many communities a growing sector of the public who have much to gain from museums. It might sound reasonable enough that people's enjoyment be diminished for the sake of future visitors, if the risks are indeed so serious and urgent, but many museum displays are actually sacrificing current enjoyment for no measurable benefit to posterity. Access to exceptionally perishable materials can be managed not only by limiting the level of light but also the duration of exposure. The traditional practice of getting visitors to lift a curtain to look at a fugitive watercolour or delicate piece of embroidery is most effective; it provides an element of dramatic surprise and protects the object against exposure to light when no one is looking at it. Modern technology can improve on such measures by sensing the approach of a visitor and raising light levels accordingly, as is done in the new Native American displays in the Field Museum, Chicago, or in the National Palace Museum in Taiwan. It is possible to adapt this technology to let people with poor sight benefit from higher levels of illumination for measurable periods of time, but this is not, as far as I know, yet being done. Rules to preserve the most vulnerable materials are being applied, blanket fashion, so that our galleries and museums are becoming distressingly dim, and short-change the visitor's experience of what is on display.

The practice of reducing light exposure in museums was prompted by the publication, in 1978, of Garry Thomson's book, *The Museum Environment*. Thomson, the Chief Scientific Officer in the Conservation Department in the National Gallery in London, set himself the task of educating museums and their public about the risks involved in putting things on display. At that time, many people both inside as well as outside museums were ignorant of the extent of the damaging effect that exposure to light and fluctuations in humidity could have. Garry Thomson decided that since any light can, theoretically, be damaging, the lowest level of light that allows people to see should be applied to all articles in museums. Research with the Barclay Institute revealed that people could still see clearly at 150 lux (an extremely low, almost crepuscular level of illumination), but Thomson felt that even that was too high an exposure for some materials, such as fugitive inks on paper or fabric. He proposed a 50-lux level for the most light sensitive substances. This level is dim by any standards, but Thomson maintained that the human eye could see well enough, if the visitor were allowed to accommodate to it, by moving through a series of chambers with decreasing illumination. Levels of 50 lux for light-sensitive material, and 150–250 lux everywhere else, have been adopted as standard for many museums, even though it is rarely possible for the museum to arrange for the slow process of visual accommodation from daylight to low levels, and colour values shift considerably at such low light levels, so that bright things appear a dismal, yellowy grey. Many pigments and supports, however, including several types of paints, inks and paper, do not require such strictly controlled conditions for the brief intervals at which they are looked at. But unless a museum curator has some training in conservation, it is very difficult for him or her to resist professional specialist advice that lighting must always be kept so low. Blanket decisions for all works on paper and for all textiles are not the answer. Museums now need to make much more subtle assessments of which objects, or even parts of objects, are at risk. And they need to assess the significance of this risk. Much light damage on old items has already occurred, and the material that remains is often comparatively stable; any further deterioration due to light is so infinitesimal as to be immeasurable by any known apparatus. Lighting need not merely be aimed at preserving the objects; it can be used to benefit the viewer. In those circumstances where light levels really have to be kept very low for most of the time, visitors could be led to them carefully so that their eyes grow accustomed, and then, if the lighting is raised to the agreed levels for the agreed length of time, the process could be dramatic and exciting, like the magical swell of an orchestra tuning up. It seems odd to have to say it, but light is essential to museums. Even art galleries, where the quality of light is obviously vital, have become dim over recent years. Tate Modern is one of the dimmest. The most beautiful light I know in a gallery anywhere in the world is in the Nordjyllands Art Museum in Aalborg, Denmark. Designed by Alvar Aalto with Jean-Jacques Baruël, the light is reflected down off curved white walls with the result that all the harmful ultraviolet rays are absorbed and the total quality of light is reduced, yet still the gallery is bathed in a glorious, luminescent glow. The same filtering system was used by James Stirling in the Clore Extension at Tate Britain, but with nothing like as effective a result. The Clore Extension was built to house the gift of paintings that Turner left to the nation after his death in 1851. His bequest contained some of his finest oils, including the majority of his radical late works, and literally thousands of luminous little watercolours in which Turner captured every conceivable transient effect of light in nature. John Ruskin, who had the unenviable task of sorting through these works in the artist's studio, stored under decades of dust, dreamed of a labyrinthine museum, with a sequence of intimate galleries for watercolours interspersed with bigger ones for oils, all beautifully lit, 'like beads upon a chain', leading the visitor through the artist's career as his capacity to capture light reached its crescendo in his later years. Here, if ever, was a chance to design a gallery as a hymn to light. Sadly, however, the Clore Extension immediately dampens one's spirits upon entering. The light in it is so subdued that the paintings look drained of colour, and all the life and love has gone out of them. Light has come to be regarded as the enemy, but it is better looked on as the gift of illumination that can lead to enlightenment.

Any access to objects can all too easily be seen by curators and conservators as a threat to their safety when, in fact, it fulfils their purpose. Those who
want to preserve things for the future and those who want to show things to
people today need to work together to find the right solutions to providing
the safest possible access to objects so that the greatest number of visitors can
enjoy them. Museums in future will need to see themselves not as bastions of
privilege, preserving their treasures for the few, but as egalitarian institutions
run by people for people. Museums can only operate on the principle that
we as human beings are one family, and much, much more alike than we are
dissimilar. Groups of chimpanzees living near each other in the jungle vary
much more greatly in their DNA than all the races of humanity. It is our
similarities that make our differences, including our excellences, so necessary
for us to understand.

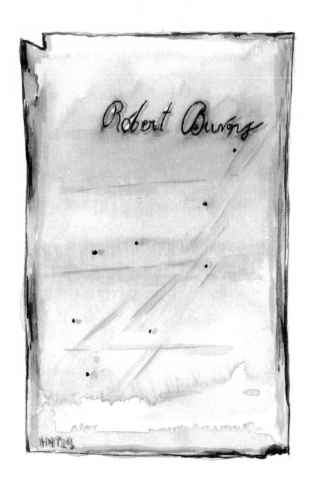

Window-pane inscribed by Robert Burns (1759–96) using a diamond-tipped
stylus given to him by his friend and patron, the Earl of Glencairn, late 18th century.
Museum of Scotland

CHAPTER SEVEN

Work and Play

People who work in museums often claim they are for everyone, but to-day it is not at all clear who they are for – the public who visit them, the researchers who use them, or the curators who work in them. In the 18th century, museums had a more unified body of users. Then everyone involved, to varying degrees, shared in the museum's ambition to extend our knowledge of the world. Though enlightenment remains the museum's main objective, the means by which this is offered to its different groups of users vary greatly. The general public want to be entertained while they learn, while scholars, at all levels of study, want to research the collections for their own purposes. The former approach is based on play, the latter on work. At the moment, curators try to serve both users at once, and fail. It is like telling someone a story while simultaneously inviting him to make up one of his own. That is what most museums try to do at present, and it is the root of so much of their ineffectiveness. To improve what they offer both general visitors and researchers, museum staff will have to change the way they work.

Nothing illustrates the current confusion between the museum's archival role and its role as a storyteller more clearly than what I call the 'white-label' disease. Most regular visitors to museums have had the frustrating experience of coming across an empty space on a wall or in a case, marked by a 'temporarily removed' notice. The most out-of-date example of this I remember seeing was in Italy in 1995. The label stated that the object had been removed, 'temporarily', in 1972. At least there was a label. The old habit of leaving gaps without any explanation has largely died out. So, too, the bizarre practice, once standard in the Walker Art Gallery, Liverpool, of taking a picture off display and re-hanging just its empty frame. But museums still think they have done their duty to visitors by telling them they cannot see something. I have yet to see a label that said when an object would be returned to display. Museums cheerily put such notices in even their most evocative settings. I once saw a splendid diorama showing a pond, complete with a hunting otter, swans resting among the reeds, a heron stalking frogs in the shallows, with the water stretching away to the other bank, merging, as it did so, into a fine painting that carried the sweep of the landscape back into the hills and high into the sky, where geese were flying. On the surface of the simulated water was a sequence of lozenge-shaped holes from which a family of ducks had been rudely plucked. Before each gaping hole, sitting on the supposed water, was a piece of folded white card informing the visitor that each of these specimens had been temporarily removed. One could never imagine white labels in a Disney park. There the visitors' needs would always come first. Museums have confused loyalties. They know they owe their visitors something, but do not think twice about taking an object off display if it is needed behind the scenes, no matter how much it depletes the visitors' experience.

Curators tend to regard their displays as open storage, while visitors see them as entertaining stories. The Egyptology Galleries at the Metropolitan Museum aim to cater for both the general public and the scholar. Behind the main public galleries are areas that are literally open stores: glass bays lined with shelves containing the department's reserve collections; in one, bales upon bales of yellowing old linen are stacked one on top of another, each discreetly numbered and labelled. Visitors sometimes wander into these dim corridors but quickly leave, unable to penetrate their meaning. Nor is the specialist well served by this arrangement, because it does not permit close examination. Open storage usually ends up satisfying neither the specialist nor the public, though many curators think that when they have created such a system, their duty to all their users is done, and they can get on with the job of curating the collection, whatever that is.

A museum is only one user of its collection; scholars from outside and members of the public both have a legitimate call on its collections, which are, after all, in public ownership. Museums tend to list, for example, only the research published by their own staff in their annual reports, but a better indicator of a museum's contribution to research would be to list all the academic research that the museum has facilitated. A museum's research function is different from its public function. There are those who come to the museum with prior knowledge and only need to be allowed into the galleries or stores to discover more, and those who come with only a slight interest and need guidance. Since a museum has to cater for these different kinds of users, it needs to be clear about the differences between its archival and its exhibition roles. Visitors to exhibitions need to see objects that will fire their imaginations; it may be a scrap of paper with a note scrawled on it by a famous hand, a massive set of chains that the Romans used to harness slaves, or a doll's cradle given to novice nuns to focus their thoughts on the baby Jesus. Scholars, however, may well value objects that have little visual impact, such as a set of accounts or a tediously similar set of moths or ball-bearings. The criteria used to create a collection for future research are different from those used to select exhibits for display.

The poet William Blake divined two contrary states in the human soul: innocence and experience. The approach of the exhibition curator benefits from innocence, the archivist from experience. Curators in charge of displays need to be able to recapture childlike wonder in order to attract the attention of new visitors. Curators in charge of research need to acquire the breadth of vision that comes with experience, to serve and anticipate the needs of all its users. Museums need two faces: one of innocent enthusiasm and the other of open-minded wisdom. Arrogant narrow-mindedness and jaded self-interest are not good for business. Knowing something and sharing it with others does not necessarily come easily, but it is essentially the job of the museum. Neither does admitting that one does not know something, but that is also essential to the work of museums. One of the most difficult things of all is to imagine not knowing something that one takes for granted. Yet this is exactly what we have to do when we try to understand the past; before people knew, for example, that blood went around the body. What would we then have thought when we felt our hearts beating? Innocence and experience are the two public faces of a museum; what they share is the collection itself. Both use it and both can add to it. This division of functions does not mean that museums need to be split into two institutions housed in separate locations, though this may be beneficial where the collections and the demands on them are considerable. Archival and exhibition services could operate well as separate departments in a larger organisation, or even as two distinct functions of one department, even of one individual, in a smaller museum. But, however it is managed, separating these two functions could open up the whole museum business so that it can serve a much broader range of users.

Anyone who has tried to gain access to a museum object in storage knows how frustrating it can be. Most museums have few resources to help with such requests, and even fewer have an efficient system for locating and retrieving things. Seeing items in store is usually granted on a grace-and-favour basis, especially to those who know a curator personally or who are working in a closely associated field. People with more distantly related interests can experience months, even years of delay, and many do not even think they have the right to ask. National collections, however, belong to everyone, and there is no reason why anyone should have to wait unreasonably or be prevented from seeing anything in store. Larger museums have, for some time now, established separate stores away from their main public buildings, for reasons of economy and space. These have tended to be managed by each institution, but it would be perfectly feasible to see the establishment of collection centres, managed on a contractual basis, as a resource for several museums, archives and other institutions with a responsibility for caring for material from the past. Even if these were not all located in one place, which would be an expensive operation, though worthwhile over time, collections could be successfully managed in several locations with the help of modern technology. No changes in ownership would be necessary (the vast majority of the material would already be in the public domain), and special access and loan conditions could be maintained by contractual agreement. Collection centres could, in time, become acquisition agencies in their own right, or, at least, recommend acquisitions that develop its holdings as a study resource, and increase access to the material in its care, both directly and through loans.

These collection centres of the future would need to be approachable places, not intimidating stores. Rather like warehouse shopping but better than that; functional and informative, spacious and easy to use, with staff to help with enquiries and illustrated catalogues and databases on computer terminals. Everyone, whether a specialist researcher or a teacher using mate-rial with a class, or anybody with an inquiring mind, would be properly ac-commodated. A model would be the Natural History Study Centre in the National Museums and Galleries of Merseyside, one of the best I have seen anywhere, where staff are available to help visitors take specimens out of drawers and study them in detail, when necessary, under a microscope. The advantage of collection centres, however, is that they would provide a single location for research. Modern approaches to history are highly contextual, taking into account all the influences that shape people's lives – from their tax bills to their health records to what they like to have about them in the home, including what they watch on television. There is going to be so much material that museums and archives will inevitably have to merge, as the records they need to preserve begin, more and more, to overlap. In fu-ture, museums will not just want to collect a mangle here and an old bicycle there; they will want to collect all kinds of evidence of the lives of the people who used these things. Collection centres with their broader approach to the past would be the best way to organise and preserve these things; too many museums currently have warehouses where the collections are dumped without even being catalogued, and public access is virtually prohibited.

Museums could then pick and choose what they want to display from col-lection centres. They would be able to draw freely from their own collec-tions, of course, but as collection centres became widely established, they would see the advantage of borrowing from others. Instead of purchasing something for themselves, they would be able to find out first if it is available on loan. If an object is already preserved for the nation, and is there to be used, then the museum could use its scarce resources for preserving some other aspect of the past, rather than duplicating what is already available. If not, they could confidently spend public money acquiring it for their own use, and then add it later to the collective pool. Collection centres would enable museums to become strategic collectors of the past, rather than creating similar, overlapping but rarely comprehensive collections, as they do now.

The great, under-used resources in museums almost everywhere are their collections. Those in Britain, viewed collectively with archives, constitute what is possibly the greatest treasure chest of history in the world. The combined public collections of America, Germany and France are not far behind. As a resource for study from primary sources, at all levels of formal and informal education, these collections have barely begun to be exploited. Making them virtually accessible, which is slowly happening, will at least let students know what is in them, but this, in turn, will lead to more requests to see real things, not just in collections separately, but across collections and curatorial disciplines. No museum has the administration to cope with such a demand at present, which is one reason for their reluctance to let people know what they have. More positively, museums could be planning today not only to meet this demand but also to stimulate it. This will require more capital expenditure, because no one in the future would dream of building a store without public study areas. But the process could begin with staff development and management change. Crucially, archives should be amalgamated with museum collections, because users need to be provided with all the evidence from the past, whatever material it is made from, and because archivists have the skills and the approach needed to unlock the vast research potential of our museum collections. Individual curators within museums think of many ways to display their collections, but usually only within the given historical framework of their museum and not in response to public need. In large, multi-disciplinary museums, it is rare to find anyone with a grasp of the scope of the collections as a whole and their potential for use and development. And no one is thinking about what the combined potential of our different museum and archive collections could be, simply because it is no one's job to do so.

Manchester and the Industrial Revolution

If you visited Manchester's museums today, you would be unlikely to discover why Mancunians used to call cotton 'King' in the 19th century. The story of how this humble plant was transformed into incredible wealth is so buried and fragmented among the city's museums that you could be forgiven for thinking that Manchester flourished without it. Even the products that were made from it are separated: the Whitworth Art Gallery collects the cloth, while the Gallery of English Costume at

Platt Hall collects the clothes that were made from this cloth. The manufacturing process is equally divided. The Museum of Science and Industry in Manchester collects the machinery that spun and wove the cotton, while the Pump House: People's History Museum collects the evidence of the people who made and worked this machinery. To see the art and artefacts on which the factory owners spent their immense wealth, you have to visit the Manchester City Art Gallery. But you will only find oil paintings there by the Pre-Raphaelite artists that these nouveau riches were so fond of collecting. To see watercolours by these artists, you have to go back to the Whitworth Art Gallery, because this institution (such are the niceties of museum collecting policies) acquires only works on paper. Hardly anywhere do you catch a glimpse of the common, foreign crop that made all this possible, or the Empire which enabled Britain to exploit it. Still less do you discover what all this amounted to: nothing less than the Industrial Revolution, which exploded into life in this city and is still rampaging through many rural economies in the world.

Now the technological revolution, with its green lawns and shrubberies and crisp office blocks, is sweeping the industrial one away. But surely there is still a point in Manchester celebrating and atoning for its famous and infamous past. It will never be able to do this if the collections that tell this story remain in bizarrely fragmented museological categories, owned and curated by several separate institutions. One way of creating a new Museum of the Industrial Revolution would be to bring all these museums together into one huge organisation, so that they could create it together. But this would present considerable management and ownership problems, almost certainly require higher levels of subsidy, and bring with it the inertia that often accompanies larger organisations, which could itself in turn mitigate against such a radical development. A less prescriptive, more organic way to enable change would be to use a collection centre as a staging post. The existence of a jointly managed though still separately owned, city-wide reserve collection would enable future museum entrepreneurs, either from within or without the current museum structure, to consider how this material could be more fully used to benefit the public. There are certainly enough artefacts currently in store in Manchester's museums to create a fascinating display about the Industrial Revolution, without diminishing the roles and individual aspirations of the existing institutions.

Devolution is gaining political momentum, as people want stronger local identities, yet wish to maintain their connections with wider national, international and global groupings. This, in turn, will influence the development of museums. They will face new pressures to tell the history of their localities, at the same time as providing a forum for international links. One can see this happening within Britain. Scotland and Wales now have some degree of political independence, and both have had, for many years, their own National Museum. But neither of these presents a unified picture of their country's history. The National Museum and Gallery of Wales, in Cardiff, has in its collection the oldest human footprints yet found on British soil. Evidence suggests that these were Welshmen. Yet the museum does not tell their story, or the story of the Welsh people. In the heart of the museum is a major display about the history of Welsh rocks. In a land famed for singing about the Land of the Fathers, visitors to the National Museum and Gallery of Wales are given the land without the fathers, and no songs. Scotland has just opened a new, purpose-built national Museum of Scotland. But it is not a museum of the whole of Scotland; it is a museum of the bits of Scottish heritage that the museum happens to have collected. The decorative arts are shown but not the corresponding fine arts, because these are collected by Scotland's National Gallery. The new museum is rather eerily empty of faces, because Scotland's National Portrait Gallery collects these. For a land famous for its poetry (what other country has adopted a poet as its national hero?), the Museum of Scotland is gravely quiet, and Robert Burns is reduced to a part-share of a showcase, represented, most evocatively, by a window-pane on which he once scratched his name. If Burns had scrawled his name across a sheet of paper this would now be an disregarded leaf in the substantial archive of his written work. But since he inscribed it on a three-dimensional pane of glass his intervention now has the status of an object, and is permanently on show in a major public museum. The Museum of Scotland is still thinking in terms of museological categories of objects, not in terms of what they mean, or how well they bring to life the history of this country for future generations. To do that the museum will have to change, as Scotland's perception of itself changes. But it has left no room for that. It is already packed. There is not even any space to expand.

Society is continually changing. The city of Bradford, once a typical Yorkshire mill town, now houses one of the largest Asian populations in Britain. In its heyday, as a capital of the wool trade, Bradford built itself a magnificent, ornate Victorian museum and art gallery, Cartwright Hall, in Lister Park, at the centre of its wealthiest residential district. Now this museum has a totally different local public, with a culture and past of its own. That culture is largely preserved in the Victoria & Albert Museum and the British Museum in London, both of which most comprehensively reflect Britain's imperial legacy, but as far as Bradford was concerned this legacy did not exist. Sustained attempts to get suitable objects out of these national museum stores and on show in Bradford have failed. In frustration, Cartwright Hall decided to build up their own collection of Asian art and historical artefacts. They discovered and commissioned much excellent material, but it would have been better if this had been done to complement major items already in public ownership. Bradford could, by now, be one of the great centres for the study and appreciation of Asian culture in Britain. This would have benefited the local population, and Britain as a whole.

Collection centres would enable those museums with a commitment to modern history to keep their collections up to date, by providing a depository for material no longer needed in their displays. The National Gallery used to select any paintings it wanted from the Tate after they were more than 50 years old, leaving the Tate free to go forward. This arrangement, which was terminated in 1998 (the National Gallery now stops its collections at 1900 and Tate Modern is seen as Britain's national gallery of modern art), was, in part, a solution to the problem that Alfred Barr identified when he began to build up the collections of the Museum of Modern Art in New York, as its first Director, in the 1930s. How could MoMA remain modern if it filled up with the past? He envisaged the museum as a 'torpedo' moving through time, with its nose pushing forward and its tail petering out in the past, as the museum sold or gave away everything it had that was more than 75 years old. Now, 75 years on, MoMA has not begun to dispose of its collection, partly for fear of offending its benefactors, partly because it goes against the grain of a museum to give anything away, but mainly for fear of losing some of its major attractions. MoMA faces a more difficult problem than the Tate because it collects everything, not just fine art. Barr was a medievalist by training and it would not have occurred to him to look at art as either 'fine' or 'decorative'. He established departments of photography, architecture and, most radically, cinema, alongside those of the so-called 'high' arts. Today, MoMA has the preeminent collections in the world in all these fields. So what is MoMA doing with all this material? Building another big extension. All that it, as well as the National Gallery and the Tate, requires is the services of a good collection centre. Then these museums would all be free to develop their collections and displays in the future, without sacrificing their duty to the past.

With Tate Modern assuming the role of our national gallery of the 20th century, there is a danger that the collection of the National Gallery itself will start to become congested, like a dammed river that no longer flows. The temptation for its curators will be to fill gaps rather than look for the next peak of achievement in the development of painting. The whole gallery could, in time, become crowded with minor works that may help explain the context of the great masterpieces, but could also dilute their power. Recent purchases at the National Gallery suggest that this has already begun to happen. Announcing its acquisition in 1998 of the *Virgin and Child* (*c.* 1265–75) attributed to the Clarisse Master, the National Gallery stated: 'not only is this painting a beautiful object in its own right, but in the context of the National Gallery's collection it represents the type of Byzantinising work from which Duccio developed'. 'Beautiful' is a fairly bold claim for this charming but rather slight panel, but does one need to know about 'Byzantinising' work to appreciate Duccio's greatness as an artist? Such a painting adds nothing to the National Gallery's artistic dimension, yet certain paintings from the 20th century could have done so. Surely the job of the National Gallery is simply to collect great paintings, whenever they were produced. Artists have not stopped painting them, so the National Gallery should not be stopped from acquiring great pictures after 1900. There will be a little overlap with the Tate's collections, but what is wrong with that? The material to draw from is so rich, and the National Gallery will only need a few splendid pictures, given their worldwide remit.

The Victoria & Albert Museum

The Victoria & Albert Museum demonstrates how a museum can become weighed down by its collection. It was founded as the South Kensington Museum in 1857 in a spirit of overwhelming optimism, 'to present to the manufacturers and the public, choice examples of what science and art have accomplished in manufactures of all kinds'. From its inception, it took an active role in encouraging interest in the arts and sciences way beyond its own walls. It played a key role in the new art education system that its founding director, Sir Henry Cole, had established, and its Circulation Department ensured that its collections reached the length and breadth of Britain. In the process of inspiring makers and teachers, the V&A developed into one the greatest museums in the world but subseqently its ambition has been shrinking. In 1893 it split into the Science Museum and the Victoria & Albert Museum, and its Circulation Department was closed in 1978. The V&A now has a major identity problem. Its efforts to keep pace with contemporary developments have often been marginal and more often national than international. It has tended to collect within old categories, and hardly begun to tackle new media. It has almost sunk beneath its own weight and its visitor figures have declined. It is no longer at the centre of British, let alone world, creativity, as it was during its early years. The museum has a choice: to rest as a great period piece, or to provide fresh inspiration for manufacturers and a wide public.

At the moment, the V&A defines itself as the world's greatest museum of the decorative arts and design, but the term decorative is inadequate when describing the work of philosophical craftsmen like William Morris or Bernard Leach, and pejorative when applied to a masterpiece of world art like the Ardebil carpet. Design is hardly a better term for, as David Hockney put it, 'the difference between art and design is that art moves you and design doesn't, unless it's a bus'. The real subjects of the V&A are visual language and visual imagination. These are universal tools of mankind, at times controlled, at others freely used, since earliest times. The great strength in the V&A lies in its breadth. It is not about art or design; it is about both. It is about art for living. Developing its reference function as a collection centre, in time in a separate building, would provide the V&A not just with the physical space, but with the intellectual space to build new collections, as an inspiration to all those who are working to enhance the visual quality of our lives today, in all walks of life, anywhere around the world. Thinking of its archival function and its display function separately would free the museum to think creatively about its identity, and rediscover its true purpose.

The creation of collection centres would change the way in which knowledge about collections is obtained and categorised. The development of the archival role of curatorship in these centres would ensure the much-needed revival of the scholar curator or, as they are called in natural history and art museums respectively, the taxonomist and the connoisseur – those people who have almost disappeared in museums, but who are vital for their future use by outsiders or by the museums themselves, simply because they know what is in the collection. No matter how powerful computers become, the human mind will always be needed to take an overview of what we know and what we need to know.

Collection centres would also need to employ conservation scientists to manage safe access, to commission restoration and, as they do in the Conservation Centre run by the National Museums and Galleries of Merseyside, show their work to the public. These staff would need to get to know the collections as a whole, but their knowledge would be different from that of the curator because it would be based on technical matters, not on interpretation. To conservators it does not matter what an object means, unless they are restoring it. Their profession requires them to treat all objects with equal respect; to preserve an object, all they have to know is how, when and of what it is made. Curators used to be responsible for acquiring this detailed technical knowledge. One only has to look at most labels in museums: they are more likely to tell you what something is made of than what it means. These categories began as simple ways of classifying material. All works on paper, whether prints or drawings, were listed together and put into folders and, later, boxes, while all works on canvas were listed separately and hung on the walls and, later, racks. This method of collecting by material made sense to museums like the V&A, which were founded to inspire craftsmen to improve their technical skills, but has little meaning to a wider public. There is a considerable disadvantage to a bed being separated from its drapes, or an oil painting on canvas from a sketch on paper made in preparation for it, just because they are made of different materials, as their meanings may be intimately related. In the late 19th century, Glasgow exchanged a collection of shipbuilding materials and methods with Japan for a collection of teapots, tableware and other domestic productions. The collection that went to Japan was used and dispersed long ago. The Japanese collection in Glasgow remained in packing cases for a century.

If the cataloguing by method of making and materials was undertaken by the conservation department in a collection centre, it could be properly researched, kept up to date, used and made accessible to the public. Since the conservation department would be also charged with the task of increasing public access to its collections, it could put on displays and publish information about the often fascinating technical discoveries it might make. This information is crucial when identifying and dating objects; for example, the date when a new pigment such as Prussian blue or a new material like nylon was introduced. If they were not tied to any curatorial discipline, conservators would be able to look at the collection from their own perspective by dividing them into say, organic and inorganic and composite materials, thereby opening up new avenues of understanding.

These collection centres would be places where people go to study the collection, leaving the museums of the future free to create the conditions that enable people to experience the collection. Curators working on displays in museums would then be able to concentrate all their attention on making a success of each visit. Thinking about what the museum is actually achieving in the visitor's mind should be the curator's special area of concern. Modern technology means that curators would begin to take over much of the communication process themselves. The material the curator has amassed while making his acquisition, the video tape of its maker or user, as well as his own commentary on the exciting moment of discovery, sound effects, music and text, would all be there at his elbow, in his own mixing suite on the computer on his desk. The curator would be able to think much more creatively through the whole museum process, from research and acquisition to display and appreciation.

Surprisingly, no one is responsible for the success of visits to museums at present, yet everyone needs to be, from the attendant at the front door to the director. Staff in museums who concentrate on benefiting their visitors should naturally become aware of all the negative factors that put visitors off, or that prevent them from fully appreciating the displays. Even if there are no barriers at the doors of a museum in the form of a dull or portentous entrance, or an officious or bored-looking individual, there can lurk a host of barriers within. These are often based on cultural assumptions that might appear so normal to staff that they may have difficulty in noticing them. If people cannot read and all the interpretation is written, these people will not want to come. If all the interpretation is in a language that some visitors do not understand, they will leave unsatisfied and will not come back again. If there are nudes on the walls, Muslims and Orthodox Jews will simply not come. If the place is deadly silent, people who like background music will be put off. If there is nothing for young children to do, families will not come. If there is nothing to interest teenagers, they will not come. If there is no access for disabled people – well, the museum can then forget this large section of the public. If the light levels are too low and the labelling too small, then people with poor sight will not come back. If there is nowhere to sit down, the elderly or infirm will not stay. If the atmosphere is oppressive or the staff aggressive, uninterested or ill-informed, then people will be quicker to leave. They will leave sooner, too, if they cannot get something to eat or drink. Above all, they will leave if they are bored, and they will never come back again.

As far as the visitors are concerned, attendants are the most important people in the museum because they are, quite simply, the only staff they usually see. It is the attendants who know most about what actually goes on in the galleries, how the public are reacting and what they are getting from their visits. Yet these are often the last people who senior museum staff think of asking about how their displays are working. Attendants are barely credited with being people at all, yet managed properly they can become one of a museum's best resources. The stereotype caricatured by Mr Bean, of a middle-aged, rather sad-looking man in uniform, falling asleep on his chair in an empty gallery, is still a widespread reality, though there are national variations on the type. In the United States, the attendants tend to be Afro-Americans and, in art galleries, at least, rather younger in age, although they often still look bored. In Russia, the attendants are almost invariably elderly women. The situation is, however, changing; more and more museums are coming to realise that they need friendly staff to help their visitors to have an enjoyable and rewarding time, and they need staff on the shop floor who can tell them how well they are really succeeding. Some of the most informative evaluation can be carried out by personal observation, and attendants are best placed to do this. Evidence of audience behaviour is often staring one in the face. In the Munch Museum in Olso the evidence is imprinted on the floor: the carpets are heavily worn in front of the most popular pictures. There is another reason for involving all staff, including attendants, in the evaluation, and therefore the decision-making process within the museum. How can museums hope to reach all sectors of the community, if they cannot communicate with the representatives of it within?

A museum exists within a community and a community exists within a museum. Both the community within the museum and the community outside it need to relate to each other if they are going to develop together. To enable this to happen, museum staff and their boards (whose job it is to see the museum is run, and not to run it) need to have a good idea of what benefits they hope the public will gain from their use of the museum, and the visitors, too, need to have some grasp of what benefits they can expect to receive. At the moment, neither have the museums a clear idea of what they have to offer, nor have the public a clear idea as to what could be on offer. The public cannot discover this for themselves. Museums have to take responsibility for the success of each visit. The collections and the public are neither first nor last. They need to be developed together.

No museum I know of works as a united team to create better and more rewarding experiences for its visitors. Fiefdoms of vested interest hold sway, in marketing, design and conservation as well as in curatorial departments, and decisions about what the museum actually does are usually the results of compromises between conflicting aims, rather than creative solutions realising a shared ambition. Museums are complex organisations, much more so than most businesses and services; they have demanding responsibilities, their customer needs vary considerably, their network of partners is often labyrinthine, and it is very difficult, if not actually impossible, to define their bottom line. Nevertheless it is up to museums themselves to make the case for the public benefit they bring, because no other institution can or will.

Two loaves on a basketwork plate, Ancient Egyptian, New Kingdom, 1550–1070 BCE.
British Museum

CHAPTER EIGHT

The Family Silver

Museums contain the most valuable objects in the world. But is there any point in seeing them in financial terms? Since they cannot be replaced, is it not better to think of them as being truly price-less? In one sense, therefore, these collections are worth nothing. But they cost money to keep and to show to the public. The crucial financial question for museums is not how much their collections are worth, but who benefits from the cost of keeping them.

Museums cannot be divorced from the communities that created and run them, and these communities vary greatly in what they want their museums to do and how much they are prepared to pay for them. Western Europe is the home of the modern museum and has treasured them consistently. But even here, the way they have done so has varied greatly from country to country. As one might expect, distinctions have followed the religious divide: Protestant countries in the north have tended to run their museums on low church lines, emphasising accessibility, education and outreach; while Catholic countries have concentrated on the primacy of the collections, and not cared too much who goes at all. In Italy there is a distinct hierarchy of subject matter, with no expense spared for works of art, while local and natural history collections often struggle to survive. In France, until recently, the hierarchy was geographical, with a handful of huge, well-endowed museums in Paris, and a host of unloved and empty little museums spread around the provinces. Germany has the most consistently immaculate museums, but the emphasis here is on education and scholarship, and public entertainment is very much a lower priority.

Outside Europe, the contrasts become greater. One can only imagine the museum Germany would have built had it happened to possess the treasures of Tutankhamun. As it is, they are housed in the Museum of Egyptian Antiquities in Cairo, and their sorry condition is a clear indicator that Egypt today is by no means fully committed to the preservation of its history. The museum is pounded daily by the traffic. It used to have its windows open so that particulate and gaseous pollution can enter freely. The result is that the treasures within, which have been beautifully preserved for centuries under mountains of stone, have deteriorated. When I visited flakes of gold lay on the lower shelves of the cases containing the Tutankhamun relics, shaken there by the eternal rumble of the traffic. An international campaign raised millions of pounds to build a new museum for these wonderful things, away from the polluted city centre, but no new museum has yet been built though the conditions in the old displays have now been improved.

It is perhaps unfair to accuse the Egyptians alone of failing to care for their past. One of the finest Ancient Egyptian collections is in Italy. The Egyptian Museum in Turin must surely rank among the worst museums in the world. Its exhibits are extraordinary, especially the entire contents of the tomb of Kha, one of the architects of the Valley of the Kings, who was interred with his wife Merit and all the provisions they would require in the afterlife, including a supply of loaves, beds made up with linen sheets, clothes for all occasions, even a spare wig. Dust lies everywhere, labels are missing, backcloths are faded and the collections themselves are disintegrating. Moreover, half of the galleries are always shut, while the guards stand in clusters, chatting amicably together. The museum is, I am told, undergoing renovation, but it has been doing that ever since I have known it, at least 30 years. Had this museum contained Italian masterpieces, the story would, I believe, have been very different. It would certainly have received the attentions of at least one leading Italian designer and a committee of conservators. But as it is, the Egyptian Museum never seems to get to the top of anyone's spending priorities. Its origins might help to explain this. It was based on the collections of Bernardino Drovetti, who was the French Consul General in Egypt in the early 19th century. Had he not happened to be Italian, his collection would probably now be in Paris. Subsequent gifts and excavations have strengthened the collections, but these have largely been of academic interest; it seems never to have caught the public's imagination or aroused any public concern.

Everything a museum collects costs money to keep. Some things cost a lot more than others. A gold ring is easy to preserve, but has to be secured against theft. A stuffed rat is less likely to be stolen (although this, mysteriously, did actually happen in Glasgow), but has to be protected from environmental damage and moths. Pictures can be cheap to hang on a wall, steam engines cost a fortune to install, and ships always need maintenance to stop them from sinking. Many enthusiasts believe that the museum's job is just to collect what they think is important and leave it to society to pay for its upkeep thereafter. But museums have to be much more responsible than that; it is their job to decide what society can afford to keep. Museums are not the only preservers of the past – much of the past is preserved *in situ*, by organisations and individuals responsible for it. Had the sculptures of the Parthenon not been taken away, no one would think of removing them now. The past needs to be integrated into our lives as much as possible, rather than channelled into central repositories. Museums have a role in concentrating attention on the significance of the past. They can enhance and explain the past but they are not its only resting place.

Collecting need not just be a financial drain, however; it can act as a major boost to the museum's economy. In 1952, Glasgow's Kelvingrove Art Gallery and Museum acquired the painting *Christ of St John of the Cross* by Salvador Dalí for £8,200. It was a huge sum in those days. There was a political storm; many argued that the money could have been better spent on housing. Since then, however, the painting has become not only one of the most popular in Glasgow, but one of the most famous religious images in the world. It has earned its cost many times over in reproduction fees alone, not to mention the number of visitors it has attracted to the city.

The economic benefits that spring from museums has been a major motive for their development in recent years. This is not a new idea. In the Middle Ages, cathedrals and monasteries vied with each other for relics, because they knew they were good for business, not just their own but those of the surrounding communities. In some cases, cathedrals even stooped to looting – 'pious theft', as it was called. In 1488, the Duomo in Perugia robbed Chiusi of the Virgin's wedding ring. They still fear a reprisal, and keep it within 15 locked boxes, stacked one inside the other, with the key to each held by a different person. Perugia flourished due to the presence of this relic, with some attributing this to the beneficent influence of the Virgin through the ring. Museums and their host cities today vie with each other to be on the cultural tourists' trail, though none, I know, would loot. No longer the subject of official veneration, and justifiably an object of contempt, the mummified body of Lenin in Moscow's Red Square would be worth preserving for its tourist potential alone. Remains of the famous are not automatic crowd-pullers; Galileo's finger lies unregarded in the Museum of the History of Science in Florence, but then that city does have a lot else to offer.

It is not surprising that countries which were subjected to colonial rule want their treasures returned, not just for reasons of national pride and to educate their citizens, but because of the growing awareness of the value of cultural tourism. Why should the imperial nations continue to benefit financially from the culture of countries they have ceased to rule? As countries develop their own cultural identity, which they are doing alongside increasing globalisation (people want to have their own roots as well as being citizens of the world), there will be mounting pressure for the return of cultural artefacts from museums in the West. Anyone who believes in the universality of culture must surely welcome this, as long as it leads to a wider understanding of world cultures, and does not merely produce nationalist ghettoes. The latter is unlikely because it contradicts the concept of cultural tourism.

And marketing needs will keep many treasures on the international stage. It would be counter-productive for countries wanting to attract tourists to turn down the opportunity to be represented in the British Museum, the Louvre or the Metropolitan Museum. The Parthenon frieze sculptures, better known as the Elgin Marbles, have surely done much more for Greek tourism on show in the British Museum, than they would have done had they stayed at home. As Greece develops its cultural tourist industry, which it has been remarkably slow to do given its assets, it might come to realise that they are best left where they are, as a major promotion for their country. After all, Greece still possesses 40 per cent of the Parthenon frieze, along with literally tons of other treasures, in their museums and museum stores, and these are more than adequate to convey the glory of their past achievements, if they could only begin to interpret them effectively.

The strongest case for the return of the Parthenon statues is based on the fact that they are part of one work of art. If a Greek nobleman had acquired the majority of the sculptures from Westminster Cathedral to save Cromwell's soldiers from smashing them to bits, we would probably now be arguing for their return, legitimately if they could be put back into their niches and the building restored to its intended splendour. But the case would be less strong if Westminster Cathedral had been blown to bits and only its shell was left standing (as happened to the Parthenon), and the sculptures would not be returned to their original setting, but merely transferred from one museum to another. It would be even less strong if our museums were already full of medieval sculptures and we were eager to attract visitors from Greece. We might then leave them on show in their splendid gallery in the heart of Athens, where they are seen every year by millions of people from around the world, only asking if we could borrow, in exchange, some examples of their own sculpture, which is little known in our country but, we understand, has some merit, too. The strongest case for keeping the Elgin Marbles in the British Museum rests on the need to have at least some museums that take a world view of the whole of history. The British Museum is one of the few capable of fulfilling that role.

It is possible that museums working amicably together, with a shared goal to increase understanding of world culture, could come to many creative, international agreements that would be in the best interests of the objects themselves and of the public. There would be many tough negotiations between them, but these are much more likely to be fruitful if they are left to curators rather than politicians. It would have been difficult to convince even the late Melina Mercouri, a former Cultural Minister of Greece and chief advocate for the return of the Marbles, of the merits of the above arguments, despite her profound interest in culture. Most politicians, however, are merely politicians. The Marbles, to them, would be just one more negotiating tool. If Britain at some stage in the future needs Greece's support in the EEC, over something like fishing rights or nuclear disposal, and the price is the return of the Elgin Marbles, they would be sent packing without further consideration, leaving the British Museum and, as a consequence, world culture substantially diminished, to the detriment, I would add, of Greece itself. The Elgin Marbles would cease to be valued for the cultural benefit they bring, but would become, for the brief period of the political negotiation, another form of coinage.

Politicians are increasingly trailing through museum collections to find icons for their cause. In 1993, Glasgow Museums received a request to return a Ghost Dance Shirt, which had reputedly been ripped from the frozen body of a Sioux Warrior killed at the Battle of Wounded Knee, the last massacre of Native American people by the immigrants. The original intention of the Wounded Knee Survivors' Association was to have the shirt buried, but they later changed their ideas and proposed that it should be shown in a museum about Wounded Knee, a museum that has yet to be built. It was also a tragic symbol of the Native American people's plight at that time, because the victims who wore them believed that the Ghost Dance Shirts would protect them from the white man's bullets. They did not. On 29 December 1890, 300 Sioux, mostly women and children, were shot dead, their corpses left to freeze in the snow. Among the many trophy-hunters who arrived at the scene in the ensuing weeks was an ex-soldier called George Crager. He managed to acquire several items of Sioux clothing, from whom we do not know, which were already valuable collectors' items at that time. Shortly afterwards, he joined Buffalo Bill's Wild West Show, as a hanger-on and translator, as it was about to set sail on what proved to be a highly successful tour of Europe. Buffalo Bill had already added the 'Battle of Wounded Knee' to its list of entertainments. The last port of call before the show returned to America was Glasgow. Just before embarking, Crager sold a collection of Sioux clothing to the museum for the princely sum of £40, equivalent to about £15,000 today. He threw in, as a gift, an item that he claimed was 'a Ghost shirt, blessed by "Short Bull", taken from a Sioux Warrior killed at the battle of Wounded Knee'. Why he did so is a mystery, since such an item, if genuine, would have been extremely valuable, especially in America, which was only weeks away.

The most likely explanation is that it was not a Ghost Dance Shirt at all, but an ordinary Sioux tunic, which Crager pretended was one, for no other reason than that he liked to spin a yarn. One of the few facts we do know about him was that he told a journalist that he had to leave the US army because of a bullet wound, which had almost cost him his arm, though his army medical record showed that this elbow injury was sustained when turning over in bed. Research confirmed that there was nothing to link this tunic with the Ghost Dance Shirt religion or Wounded Knee; it did not look like other Ghost Dance Shirts, which are remarkable and ghost-like (– though some ordinary tunics were blessed to serve as them), there were no signs of bullet holes, no traces of blood, and certainly no evidence of it having been pulled from a frozen corpse. But the politicians on both sides in the 1990s were entirely uninterested in the question of authenticity. The future of the Ghost Dance Shirt was not their concern.

The Wounded Knee Survivors' Association was concerned with attracting publicity for their land rights issues, and the politicians in Glasgow, by associating with an exploited native people, were airing their credentials to be elected to the newly devolved Scottish Parliament. An 'open' meeting was held to gauge public opinion, though the audience were not allowed to contribute. They had to sit back and listen to the set speeches, one of which was in Gaelic. At the end of the meeting Glasgow was presented with a more ghastly than ghostly, fluffy white replica of the Shirt, and in 1999 the dubious relic itself, with a fanfare of publicity, was ceremonially handed over at a Wopila Tonka, a great thanksgiving. Throughout this long and sorry farce, the one thing that was forgotten was the shirt itself, and the benefit it could bring to the people who saw it. It would certainly do more to raise awareness of Native American issues in Europe, where such items are comparatively rare, than it would in America, where even indisputably original Ghost Dance Shirts are numerous (and incidentally, certainly available to be shown at any future museum about Wounded Knee). Museum curators could have sorted all this out among themselves, without any interference from politicians. Any transfer of cultural property can only be justified if it increases national and international understanding of culture. It cannot be valued in terms of political advantage, or financial gain.

The impact of a museum or art gallery on the wider economy, however, has to be considered as a factor of its own economy. Glasgow was the first post-industrial city to rebuild itself on the back of an art gallery. Though the City invested £22 million housing the Burrell Collection, and spends £2 million a year running it, the economic spin-off for Glasgow has been enormous, not just in terms of tourism but in transforming the city's image from being one of the poorest, most deprived conurbations in Europe, into a dynamic place, good to live in and good for investment. Analysis shows that the museums in Glasgow contribute about £40 million a year (this figure, some economists maintain, could be twice as high) to the economy of the city, by encouraging tourist-related expenditure and inward investment to Glasgow, over and above the employment they provide directly and indirectly. Glasgow museums cost £13 million a year to run. They attract three million visitors. So the subsidy per visit is approximately £4.30, which is good value in relation to the cost of most public services. But if you add to this the economic benefits the museums bring to the city, visitors are not being subsidised at all, but are earning the city substantial sums of money!

The new Guggenheim Museum is Bilbao's Burrell Collection. It was paid for by Bilbao as a calculated attempt to attract more tourists and inward investment to the city, after a period of depression following the closure of many heavy industries. It has been hugely successful, like the Burrell Collection. It is regarded locally as something of a cultural imposition. It is not actually a museum but, like Tate Modern, a temporary exhibition space for its parent body, in this case an ocean away, not just upstream. It does not collect itself, but houses loan collections of mostly American art and temporary exhibitions organised by its parent body, the Guggenheim Museum in New York. Bilbao is bidding for the return of Picasso's *Guernica* from Madrid, as an icon of the Basque people's historical independence. This would certainly give the new museum a local relevance, if it were shown there, and not in Guernica itself, which is also asking for its return. But, at the moment, only the building is local to Bilbao. The contents' owners are across the Atlantic.

Time will tell whether or not this new Guggenheim will prove not just internationally eye-catching but beneficial, too, to the people of Bilbao. Without their support, it will be a difficult project to sustain. The new gallery cost £70 million to build. After one year, its local attendance has dropped by half, though its foreign visitors have gone on increasing, attracted in part by the exhibition programme that comes from New York and therefore benefits from the wealth, corporate sponsorship and tax concessions of the American economy, which would otherwise be inaccessible in Europe. The new gallery attracted a million visitors in its first year and, although the numbers have since fallen, the gallery's budget was based on income from 485,000 visitors, so it is well cushioned. The long-term future of the gallery may not be significant, however. In five or ten years' time, the museum is likely to have fulfilled its purpose, in terms of the local economy. It has already put Bilbao on the tourist map, where it was not before. Politics played a major part in this museum's inception; more, I think, than the desire to promote art. Much has been made of the economic impact of cultural expenditure, but much more important are its cultural benefits.

The Guggenheim Museum in Bilbao is only a success because it is a work of architectural genius that has caught the world's imagination. It is an exception, not a rule. As I write, all over Britain, exotic heritage attractions, many clad in metal, are appearing on vacant lots, like a fleet of crashed space-ships, paid for by the National Lottery. If they all succeed in attracting all the visitors their business plans require, every person in Britain will have to spend four weeks of the year visiting them (currently they spend four days in heritage-type attractions). Clearly that is impossible, even if every building were a Bilbao. The fundamental flaw in the Lottery strategy was that money was available for building but not running costs – each project had to earn its keep. Local councils everywhere, to attract capital investment to their communities, turned a blind eye to optimistic income projections. Billions of pounds of public money has therefore been wasted on projects that were little more than wishful thinking when, with those sums, many really worthwhile ventures could have been launched which would have brought lasting benefit.

The National Centre for Popular Music in Sheffield had the unenviable record of being the first Lottery project to open and the first to close. It lasted 11 months, having cost £15 million. The project failed simply because there was nothing of any substance in it, not even music, only a mêlée of snatches, which were presumably the only performing rights they could afford. There was, of course, an interactive area where kids could make a lot of noise, to no apparent purpose, and visitors could try singing against backing tracks of poorer quality than the average karaoke. The nadir of the experience was the hall of history – an overview of the last 50 years of popular music represented by a sequence of Ken and Barbie dolls dressed, in badly stitched costumes, as skinheads, rockers, goths, New Age travellers and punks. It was not surprising that few visitors paid to go in, and none returned. The National Centre for Popular Music closed the same year that the EMP (Experience Music Project) opened in Seattle, in a building designed by Frank Gehry. EMP is entertaining but it has serious aims. For a start it is based around something substantial; it contains the world's largest collection of Jimi Hendrix memorabilia, and other relics such as Muddy Waters' guitar. Even more important, it includes a considerable and growing library of oral histories that put pop music into its personal, historical and social context. If any country merits a museum of pop music (let alone a museum of popular culture as a whole), apart from the United States, it is Britain. The National Centre for Popular Music failed because it was not properly thought through, nor did it get adequate support. The museum community as a whole must take some responsibility for this, in their failure to collect the history of this major aspect of modern life, that could have provided the core around which such a national centre could have been built. Instead, it has been left to the restaurant chain, Planet Hollywood, to buy up all this material, and Britain's National Centre for Popular Music has been turned into a nightclub.

What the Lottery has revealed is the absence of any national strategy for museums in Britain. While the Museum of the Moving Image, arguably the most important museum of recent film history in Britain, had to close for lack of funds, and the V&A failed to get support to show its 20th-century collections, £20.75 million of Lottery money was found to open the Gilbert Collection in Somerset House, a sumptuous new museum for a collection of rich men's ornaments from the 18th and 19th centuries – an area of collecting in which Britain is already well endowed. The museum contains a replica of Sir Arthur Gilbert's office in America, complete with a waxwork of the collector himself, wearing his usual primrose tennis kit and trainers, sitting behind his marble and ebonised wood, hard-stone and gilt-bronze bureau (Florence, c.1840–60). Smiling, he talks for eternity into the phone, presumably clinching the purchase of yet another excruciating example of the bastardisation of the Roman mosaic master's art that so notably grace his collection, such as the late 20th-century tableau of blue-eyed boys in rags befriending doe-eyed puppies called *Two Little Tykes*. When he saw the reconstructed office, Sir Arthur complained that it was too small. He was right. Its intimacy lends him a false humility. Had it been replicated at full scale, as he had requested, the vacuity of the whole enterprise would have been more apparent. Supporters of the Gilbert Collection claim that only the capital costs have been spent, and much of that has been used to open up Somerset House for public use; the running costs will be earned through income at the door. It remains to be seen if they will. If not, the public will be obliged to subsidise a collection the British do not need.

Governments will always want to pay as little as possible for their museums. Their stringency can be stimulating, but not if the basic level of support falls so low, as has happened recently to museums in Britain, apart from a few Nationals, that staff become demoralised. Sponsorship has been heralded in recent years as a source of alternative funding for museums, particularly by governments that are intent on reducing public expenditure in all fields. The idea has been that sponsorship raised from the private sector will reduce a museum's dependence on the public purse. The lie to this is given by the fact that it is the museums which receive the highest government subsidy that attract the most sponsorship. Sponsorship usually comes from businesses interested in using it as a form of marketing. Individual gifts do not necessarily indicate real support what the organisation is trying to achieve. A sponsor of the Los Angeles Opera once frankly admitted that 'it's so wonderful to support the Opera because they hold such wonderful parties and you meet such interesting people and you do not have to go to the opera'. It is hardly surprising, then, that sponsors favour the most successful institutions, and they are usually the ones who are the best endowed. At first sight, the exception appears to be America, where private funding is more successful and widespread, but this is only because individuals can determine to a much greater extent how they pay their taxes. They can claim tax relief for donations to a museum or other charity, which means that much more of the American museum sector is publicly funded than may first appear, even if these funds do not reach the museum via the treasury.

Wherever museums are in the world, from America to China, none that I know of are run at a profit. They are all subsidised by individuals or, more usually, by the state. Societies that just pay lip service to their museums will subsidise the preservation of their collections, but everything else, including access and exhibitions, will have to be paid for by the people who use them, or by sponsorship. Mrs Thatcher went further than that, in private at least, if not in public. She told Sir David Wilson, then Director of the British Museum, that if he had money problems he should sell some of the things he had in his stores. It is essential for museums that society values their collections, but can a price be put on this value? A painting by Van Gogh could only be said to be worth £25 million if that sum could buy an equivalent experience for everyone who will look at it. A Van Gogh bought at that price would only need to be hanging in the National Gallery in London for just over 10 years, for the sight of it to cost each visitor 50 pence. Fifty pence to see an original Van Gogh seems good value to me. And the cost per sighting would diminish increasingly ever after. Items that enter public collections effectively cease to have any financial value because they are not acquired to be re-sold; their value is in their meaning. Museums can resist threats to sell off their collection by operating not in isolation, but as a community of museums that collectively preserve the past. Such action is the best safety net for the past. There has to be a system for protecting the past against the vagaries of fashion (and politics), while allowing for deeper shifts of interest in culture. Collection centres would provide the long-term repositories for objects that are no longer needed for immediate display.

Once a society has accepted that it needs to spend money looking after its past, it has to decide who it wants to benefit from this expenditure. Should the emphasis be placed on spending public money for those who already know a great deal about history or the arts and sciences, or for those who know little or nothing but might, given encouragement, become interested? It is in the long-term interest of a society to subsidise those who are not yet participating in its culture. People who know a lot about some aspect of the past and know their way around the museum, also know how to get all they want out of it. Since they bring their knowledge with them, the museum can economise on its presentation to them. They can be effectively catered for in a collection centre. More thought and funding needs to be directed towards those who require the help of the museum to get them started. Every visitor's contact with an exhibit is an opportunity for his or her cultural development. The museum has to focus its resources on these encounters rather than on work that takes place behind the scenes. The question is, who pays for these encounters? Since it is a principle in civilised countries that education needs to be free and museums are, primarily, educational organisations, the subsidies they receive should be directed towards their wider educational role.

During the debate over entrance charges that raged through Britain in the 1980s and 1990s, it was argued by the pro-chargers that the cushioning of state support encouraged museums to become complacent about their public and indifferent to their audience's needs and interests. If entrance charges were levied, it was argued, a museum would inevitably become more attentive to its visitors' needs. But this does not necessarily happen. Some charging museums pay lip service to audience development by only putting on shows with obvious popular appeal, so automated dinosaurs do the rounds. Others, however, do not seem to mind seeing their visitor numbers decline; the staff in them can then pursue their own concerns in peace. A museum's attitude towards its public is not determined by whether or not it charges an entrance fee but by the attitude of its staff. I well remember, in 1985, going to see Sir Roy Strong, then Director of the V&A, to try to persuade him not to introduce voluntary entrance charges. The V&A was enjoying attendances of over two million a year in those days, well over half of these coming from Britain. He assured me that welfare-state museums were a thing of the past. My arguments failed to make him change his mind, though he had the decency to listen to my case. A voluntary charge, whatever that is, was introduced, followed nearly a decade later by one that was compulsory. In 1997, UK attendance at the V&A had dropped to 400,000 visits per year, many of these being repeat visits by local residents who had joined the Friends' scheme and some only coming in for tea. Measured in terms of the whole UK population, the V&A's national visibility had shrunk virtually to zero. Sir Roy Strong underestimated the degree to which his museum relied on public subsidy. It could never break even, let alone become profitable. A recent survey of public museums in the United States that levy an entrance charge, showed that out of the 130 surveyed, only a third earned more than 4 per cent of their operating expenses from charging. Even the Metropolitan Museum of Art, in the centre of New York, earns only 16 per cent of its colossal $74 million running costs from entrance charges. It is one of a handful of public museums, most of them on tourist routes, whose earnings from ticket sales are more than 10 per cent of their operating cost. All public museums are heavily subsidised, even in the States. Sir Roy Strong was wrong: the welfare-state museum is here to stay, and to be built upon.

It is a simple fact, confirmed by all the evidence, that museums which charge attract an average 40 per cent fewer visitors than they would if they were free. And this is not just a one-off drop in attendance immediately following the introduction of tickets. With very few exceptions, and without major changes in circumstances, museums that start charging do not regain the audiences they had when they were free. Between 1987 and 1997, visits to free museums increased by 28 per cent, while visits to charging museums declined by 13 per cent. It stands to reason that a free museum will have more visitors than one that charges. It would be odd if it did not. The reduction in numbers at a charging museum is significant politically as well as economically. The state pays for the museum to exist. Before the V&A introduced charges it attracted over 2 million visitors a year, at a subsidy of about £14 per visit. When it began to charge, its total visitor figures halved, and the public subsidy per head went up to over £21 – that is, after the visitors' contribution to the running of the museum had been deducted! The V&A became the most expensive state-run museum in Britain, as far as its value per visitor was concerned. It just topped the Natural History Museum and the National Maritime Museum, which each cost £19 per head. The next most expensive were the Imperial War Museum and the Science Museum – the latter with substantial attractions outside London, which almost doubled its visitor numbers. These cost £8.50 per head. All these were charging museums and they cost substantially more per head than comparable free entry museums: the Tate, the British Museum and the National Gallery were subsidised to the tune of £6.30, £5.50 and £4.10 per visit respectively. This meant that the state ended up paying more for each visit to a museum that charged than it did for each visit to a museum that was free.

Even more important than the economic argument, however, is the social one. Not only do the numbers decline when a museum starts to charge, but the social reach of the museum declines, too. Those who are put off by charges are the less well-off, particularly those who live further away and have families. Regular visitors who liked to pop in just to see a few things are disinclined to do so any more. Also put off (and this is a very important group for the museum) are those who are not motivated to go at all, but might be persuaded by a friend or a chance circumstance to try out a museum visit, if it were free. Among these must be a great many youngsters, like the rather reluctant friends I took to museums to share my enthusiasm when I was a boy. These are the potential new audiences that the museum has to do everything it can to attract, and without whom its long-term future is doomed. If about half its potential visitors are discouraged, the audience a charging museum is left with is made up of the better off, especially those who live nearby, since museums are often located in central or wealthy neighbourhoods; specialists, who often through their contacts do not pay anyway; and tourists. In a charging museum, therefore, the public funding goes to the better off, whereas the people who need that investment, the poor and the not yet interested, are left without any encouragement to visit. Most museum collections contain gifts that have been left to benefit the whole of society, not just part of it. Free museums are welcoming by nature; charging museums of necessity make you think twice before entering. There is no way of knowing how many would-be visitors turn away at the door of a museum because they are not sure that the cost of going in will be worth it. The greatest group of museums in the world, collectively known as the Smithsonian Institution, in Washington DC, has a policy of providing free access for all. So does the wealthiest museum in the world, the J Paul Getty Museum in California. All public museums should aspire to be free, not as a matter of principle but as a vision.

It is, in fact, often better economics for a museum not to charge entry. Shops do not charge people entry, and so it can be with museums. By keeping the museum free at the door, and by attracting more people in, the museum can persuade people to part with their money in the temporary exhibition, in the shops and café and on various special services, whilst ensuring that the collections are accessible to everyone. Charging museums lose out on this; people are reluctant to pay twice and so temporary exhibitions inside generally have to be free, and there are fewer visitors anyway to spend in the shop and the café. All the exhibitions in the Metropolitan Museum in New York are free because people now have to pay to come in at the door. Free museums are the healthiest and happiest museums, both socially and economically, because the money they receive is freely given by its users, and by a society which is happy that its money benefits all of its members and not just a few.

Many would agree that everyone in a community who pays for a museum should be able to get into it free. But they baulk at the idea of providing such a service free for tourists as well, particularly those who come from wealthier countries than their own. But it is difficult to charge tourists and allow local people to come in free. The local people therefore have the onus of identifying themselves. Tourists can be charged for audio guides and encouraged to spend more in the shop and café, where there can also be two pricing structures, one for visitors and one for locals, as is now common in Russia. In Britain many in the tourist industry are against museums charging at all. We may not have the best weather or the best beaches in the world, but we do have some of the best museums, and many of them are still free. Museums are one of Britain's main attractions, and providing them free is that extra something that makes a difference and costs the country effectively nothing at all in relation to the income earned from tourism. In fact, the free museum policy possibly makes more income for Britain than it costs because of the increased numbers of tourists it attracts. Tourism has an increasingly important role to play in many economies, but this does not mean that a country has to milk the tourist of everything they have. The country needs to give the tourist something in return for his or her visit. Free museums, where a culture's past is part of its living development, will not be just full of other tourists, but places where local people welcome tourists and where tourists feel welcome. According to one survey, over 80 per cent of tourists visit a local museum. This is a remarkably high percentage and offers tremendous potential for museums to develop services that satisfy these visitors. But remarkably few do. And it is not only the smallest museums that fail to make the effort; virtually no label in the Louvre recognises the existence of any other language but French. Tourists in the 19th century were called explorers; travellers still have a similar motivation although they have an easier time of it. The truth is that not all tourists are multilingual and rich, and museums in the long term cannot afford to turn away people who are visiting from abroad, particularly if they are young. I once watched, with sadness, two students counting up their money to see if they had enough to get into the V&A, before they turned away.

It is not just the visitors that change after a museum introduces charges; the whole museum can change as well. Its attention can become focused on the numbers of people who are paying the one-off sum at the door. The museum feels it has to give them their money's worth, a good ride for their ticket; one they can measure, which ensures a maximum through-put and money earned. And it often is, literally, a ride; in a car, or on foot, through an experience that has a beginning, middle and end, which leaves the visitor enthralled and excited by what he or she has seen and felt and learned, and cannot wait to tell his or her friends, and come back with them again, when they can afford it. This is fine; indeed, this is exactly what museums have to learn to do: to tell stories that enthral a wide public. But the economics of the entry charges ensure that each visit is a one-off, full-length experience, like a film or play. It is a visit that lasts, say, less than two hours and can be done in one go. This might be all right for small attractions and for temporary exhibitions but can you do – and should we want others to do – the V&A, or the British Museum, or the Louvre, for that matter, in one go? Museums do not function like cinemas or funfairs. They are more like gardens, historic quarters of a town, a book of poems or an encyclopaedia. They are somewhere one wants to browse and explore and return to, again and again, always discovering something new.

The Museum of Maquettes, Pietrasanta, Italy

Most museums in Italy charge an entrance fee, are badly maintained and empty of visitors, with their displays notoriously inadequately interpreted. The exceptions are those on the main tourist route, which suffer from all the above shortcomings except for the lack of visitors. In Pietrasanta, however, the situation is different. This is the small town near the Carrara marble quarries, where stonemasons and bronze casters work for artists, many of whom stay in the vicinity while their pieces are being made. The town has a small museum of original maquettes and models that artists have given to the community after the full-sized works have been carved or cast. This museum is open free of charge to all who wish to see it, and it provides a library and information about the artists and the workshop processes involved as well. The town also holds regular exhibitions in a fine old church off the Piazza del Duomo, and in the Piazza itself, also free. There is a sense here of art and life, of the past and the present coming together and interrelating in a way that I have found nowhere else in Italy, despite the huge potential it has for creating just such relationships. It is significant that the idea to create the Museum of Maquettes came from an outsider. Jette Sorenson, the wife of a Danish sculptor working in the town, could not believe that all the artists who worked there left without leaving a trace, coming as she did from a culture where even the smallest community has an art gallery as if by right. It was only her persistence and years of dedication that created the museum in Pietrasanta, but the town now appears to have taken it to its heart. Pietrasanta is a model for others. Its economy is based on art but it generously puts something of its commerce back into society, and the key to that is the open-door policy of the town's museum.

The great public museums of the 19th and early 20th century grew because they were rooted in the lives of their communities. The magnificence of their growth indicates the depth of their roots. Few sights in civic architecture equal London's Natural History Museum, Cardiff's National Museum and Gallery of Wales or Glasgow's Kelvingrove Museum and Art Gallery, with its vast central hall where the organ plays every Sunday as crowds of families gather. These buildings are a confident demonstration of the importance of culture and a belief in widespread access to learning. They were not additions to society but integral expressions of it. Museums foster personal development and cultural identity. They are places where people feel at home, where they can come and go, where they can absorb the past and find expression for their feelings, where they take their children and their children, in time, take theirs. Through this regular use by people throughout their lives, from one generation to another, museums become part of the public realm. They are not places you visit, but places you live with. They provide homes for our memories and palaces for our imaginations. No one in society need feel excluded. How then can museums bear to know – as all those that charge entry have to – that they will never see 80 per cent of their visitors again? Museums are a collective responsibility and need to be paid for collectively.

This chapter has been about money, although money has rarely been mentioned. Museums are not business operations. Their bottom line cannot be measured in terms of expenditure and income, profit and loss. They do not produce a commodity that can be sold and become the possession of someone else. In that strict sense, they cannot be privatised. The family silver cannot be sold without the family itself, in some crucial way, becoming depleted. The commodity that museums provide, if the benefits they bring have to be viewed in that way, are deeper and longer lasting than the individual experiences that visitors take away with them. Museums provide a collective resource that it is impossible to place a value on, but which we have come to feel is vital to our culture and to civilisation itself. Once one is aware of this, the selection of what goes into our museums becomes much more demanding. The chosen items need to reflect a general need, but cannot be chosen by everyone. Curators have to be responsive to general needs, not just their own, when acquiring works for a public collection.

Though museum collections cannot be valued meaningfully in financial terms, they do cost money to buy, keep and show, as every treasury official and politician knows. Museums need to be aware what their price is, but they should not feel constrained by it. They will never represent more than a minuscule fraction of any state's total expenditure, so they need never fear that they are costing too much. The cultural, educational and economic benefits they bring far outweigh their cost, so they can always bid for development with confidence. Museums can take heart from the fact that societies tend to look after their heritage even in the most stricken circumstances. They will always hang onto the family silver rather than sell it.

Hermit crab (*Cenobita Diogenes*) occupying the shell of a marbled turbo (*Turbo Marmaratus*).

CHAPTER NINE
Borrowed Robes

Museums in the 18th century had no doubts about what they should look like. Since they were about the past, they simply borrowed their identity from the past, usually from the age most admired for its spirit of inquiry, its artistic expression and its sense of justice for mankind: Greece *c.*5th-century BCE. The classical temple became the favoured form for all museums, but it also became the favoured form for banks, town halls and law courts; for any institution, in fact, that aspired to unimpeachable status. In our times there has been a vast amount of new museum building all around the world but it is difficult to think immediately of one that tells you, by its appearance alone, that it is a museum. There is no modern image for a museum.

John Ruskin, who did so much to stimulate the Gothic Revival in the Victorian Age, later complained of the inadequacy of almost all 19th-century buildings in the Gothic style. They failed, he thought, to capture the spirit of the original. He wrote: 'it is easy to carve capitals on models known for a thousand years, and impossible to fail in the application of mechanical methods and formalised rules. But it is not possible to appeal vigorously to new canons of judgment without the chance of giving offence; nor to summon into service the various phases of human temper and intelligence, without occasionally finding the temper rough and the intelligence feeble.' He was complaining of the mechanical aspect of so much of the detail of Gothic Revival architecture. This was, he felt, because the craftsmen's minds and hearts were not engaged in the act of creation. Ruskin believed that 'architectural ornamentation should be executed by the men who design it, and should be of various degrees of excellence, admitting and therefore exciting the intelligent co-operation of various classes of workmen'. Is a museum built not for a museum but by it, too fanciful an ambition, so that the architect of the future is part of a group within the museum who find their intelligent co-operation admitted and excited? Might this not result in museum buildings that suggest all the interesting things that are going on within? The poetry of a museum would not, then, be confined to its content but also flood through its form. If that could happen, a new age of museum building could be born.

During the last quarter of a century there has been an unprecedented explosion in museum-building around the world. New museums are springing up everywhere from India to Japan, from New Zealand to Brazil. Six hundred have opened in America alone since 1970, bringing the total in that country up to at least six thousand. There are no fewer than five national museums being opened, as I write, in Singapore. New Zealand has just opened a new, ambitious and extremely successful Te Papa Tangarewa Museum of New Zealand. There are museums being designed at the present time that deal with glaciers in France, world religions in Taiwan and computer games in Japan. Saudi Arabia has just launched the Abdulaziz Historical Centre in Riyadh. It is as big as the new Getty Museum in Los Angeles and comprises a Natural History Museum, including early archaeological material, a Historical Museum covering the history of the State since the birth of the Prophet, and a Gallery of Modern Art, that is closed for religious reasons. The Centre was created to coincide with the legalisation of foreign tourism in 1999, but it is still managed according to the Islamic codes: women and men are allowed in on alternate days, families at weekends. Even in a country where all public performances, including the cinema, are illegal, museums can flourish.

It could truly be said that we are living in a Museum Age. And as they did with cathedrals in the past, leading architects are ambitions to build them. I.M. Pei, Richard Rogers, Norman Foster, Richard Meier, Renzo Piano, Hans Hollein, James Stirling, Frank Gehry, Daniel Libeskind – and that is only the beginning of the roll-call – have all designed famous museums. The Pompidou Centre, the Pyramid at the Louvre, the Getty Museum in Los Angeles, the Jewish Museum in Berlin and the Guggenheim Museum in Bilbao are rapidly becoming icons of our times. Surveying modern museums and galleries is like looking at a panoply of the world's most famous architectural talents. It is, however, essentially their creativity that is on display, not that of the museum. Architects look on museums as ideal commissions for prompting magazine coverage and making a mark in their profession, because museum curators are usually concerned only with the interiors and leave the architect free to do what they like with the external appearance. Sometimes the architect's expressive ambitions can chime with the needs of the museum. Frank Gehry's new Guggenheim Museum in Bilbao does this. He has created a building that looks like a gigantic, dissected and partly distended, titanium-clad snail; more sculpture than architecture. It appears totally dysfunctional and is therefore an apt expression of its contents. Most people looking at it probably guess that it is a modern art gallery simply because it would be difficult to think what else it could be.

Frank Gehry was greatly influenced by Californian roadside cafés, which are often designed to look like the food they serve. One of his first buildings, for which he developed the scale-like forms that have flourished with such exuberance in Bilbao, was a Japanese restaurant specialising in fish. The Bilbao Guggenheim was conceived of as a marketing tool as well as a work of art. In doing so, it is only expanding the brand established by its parent body, the Guggenheim Museum in New York. Frank Lloyd Wright's world-famous building was designed to stand out; it is squat and curved in a town where everything else is tall and straight. Inside, the building is more of an architect's revenge on art, than a paean of praise to it. How can one hang pictures and place sculptures in a space where the walls all curve and the floors all slope? Lloyd Wright wanted to be the only artist in his buildings; he left no space for the occupants to express their own taste, let alone show other artists' work. Modern installation artists now welcome the Guggenheim's interior as a space to vie with, not merely a backdrop. Frank Lloyd Wright has got what he wanted: the architect enjoying equal status with the artist; but could he have anticipated such a victory?

Now, many museums are trying to re-launch themselves on the back of a memorable piece of modern architecture, whatever the content. Nobody seeing the model for the proposed extension to the Victoria & Albert Museum in London, when it was first presented to the public, could have had a clue what it would be like inside. Daniel Libeskind's building appeared to be a disjointed jumble of interlocking boxes, a crazy excrescence along a distinguished boulevard, another one of the Prince of Wales's notorious 'carbuncles'. It was difficult to imagine how pictures could be hung in it or what the displays would look like because there was, from the outside, not a vertical wall in sight. Nor was there, at first, any clear presentation of how it would be used or what it was for, except for the general statement that the museum needed a modern wing to house its modern collections. To the public, the proposal looked like yet another architect seeking attention, and the project failed to get support from the National Lottery. Despite this, the V&A are still campaigning to get it built, but they will only be successful if they can make its purpose clear. If used not to fossilise its 20th-century holdings but as a location within the V&A to enable it to keep perpetually in touch with the present, the building could play a really dynamic role in the life of the museum, and become not just the final infill in the quadrangle, but the diamond that sets the whole ring sparkling.

The J Paul Getty Museum, Los Angeles

The new Getty Museum, designed by Richard Meier, gives the impression that it could be a corporate headquarters when one first sees its vast, block-like structure high on the hill overlooking Los Angeles; it does not say 'museum' at all. The Getty Museum, with nearly limitless money at its disposal, has not given us a new architectural vision of a museum.

The trustees of the Getty can hardly be blamed for this, because that is not what they set out to do. Their intentions were more modest, though clear and admirable; they wanted to ensure that the works of art could communicate as directly as possible to the visitor, that the museum as a whole would provide an uplifting experience and that all relevant background information about the exhibits would be made available. They chose to treat these three aims separately. The paintings are displayed in a traditional manner, in rooms which remind one of the National Gallery in London, almost all well-spaced and hung on the line in daylight that is reflected down the tall rooms so effectively that there are no irritating frame shadows. Each picture is bathed in just the right amount of light to ensure that the whole range of its hues and tones are clearly visible. This in itself is no small achievement. Next to the galleries showing the works of art, but separate from them, are more intimate spaces filled with computers and literature for those who want to study the collections in greater depth.

The uplifting aspect of the ensemble as a whole has been left to the architect and the setting. The site itself could not be more elevating, and effectively does the job on its own. In whatever direction you look from the gleaming white plaza, though surrounded by white building-blocks of varying geometry, pierced by huge sheets of glass, and linked by glazed walkways in the sky, you catch glimpses of the vast city miles below and the Pacific Ocean stretching far to the horizon. What is strange, however, is the difficulty one has, when standing in the blazing sunshine on the Getty mountain, to remember what the buildings look like inside, and conversely, when standing inside them, what they are like outside. Walking through the cool air-conditioned galleries, one could be in a museum anywhere in the world, most likely in Europe. Standing outside, you are bathed in the heat of the Californian sunshine, and battered by the warm Californian wind, and the galleries you have just walked through could be an air flight away. The Getty Museum wears the clothes of current corporate design while its interior is taken from the art galleries of 18th- and 19th-century Europe. In some ways, it has not progressed much further than the Uffizi Gallery in Florence (though some may congratulate its creators on this), which served originally as the head office for the Medici's family business, with a display of their magnificent art collection on the top floor.

The absence of any desire to proclaim to the outside world what they are about is one reason why so many museums choose to house their collections in converted premises. Like hermit crabs they scuttle to hide their sensitive backsides in the nearest vacant shell. There are economic reasons for this, though conversions can often, in the end, be as expensive as new build, if not more so. There are opportunistic reasons for choosing existing premises, too. If no other use can be found for old buildings that merit preservation, someone usually comes up with the idea of turning them into museums. In that way many museums have found themselves located in fine buildings in city centre sites, but with quite unsuitable display conditions, insurmountable problems with circulation and an external appearance that might be of historic value in itself but seldom chimes with the museum's purpose. An exception is Jeshajahu Weinberg's Museum of the History of Jerusalem, housed in the ancient Tower of David. As a visitor, you weave your way through from one display to another, along corridors and up flights of stairs, along battlements and over courtyards, until you are led up to the top of the tower itself where there is an unforgettable view of the compact, ancient city spread beneath you like a glowing bowl of history in the hills. This view is the most precious item in the museum. It brings to life all you have learned in the displays. Suddenly the sacking of the Temple is real, because there are the vast ruins of it at your feet. The history you have learned is no longer academic, but tangible. An old building is of greatest value to a museum if it serves as a real object which helps the museum achieve its objective.

The Castelvecchio Museum in Verona

Few conversions have been as brilliantly successful as Carlo Scarpa's re-modelling of the Castelvecchio in Verona in 1964, although the castle itself has little to do with the contents, and would have told a very different story if developed as a museum about itself. In this unlikely setting, Scarpa achieved a masterpiece of design that has influenced art gallery display, both throughout Italy and abroad. The museum's collection of medieval and Renaissance painting and sculpture is beautifully and imaginatively positioned throughout the building, with wonderful shafts of light falling on objects at just the right moment, catching the tip of an angel's wing or throwing the shadowy profile of a Madonna across the floor. The vistas are particularly impressive and arresting; as you round a corner, you repeatedly come across the unexpected: the back of a statue, draped in a swathe of hanging robes, never intended to be seen but, nevertheless, a magnificent display of the sculptor's craft; a picture stand-ing on an easel at a surprising angle in the corner of a room; a vista up a flight of stairs; a sudden view across a courtyard. Everything has been thought about and beautifully spaced; every surface and material has been considered: rough stone then plaster, wood then metal. The light in the space seems to acquire a material significance of its own; it embraces the works of art with beauty. And by doing so it transforms what is es-sentially a rather run-of-the-mill collection into something much greater than its parts. The works of art cease to communicate their original meaning, as warnings of retribution or promises of heaven, and become objects of purely aesthetic delight. In Carlo Scarpa's hands, the whole museum becomes a work of art. Showing an object in its 'best' light is, in itself, a form of interpretation and tends to reveal the taste of its own times rather than the times from which the object came. Carlo Scarpa's interior already has a 1960s look, though none the worse for that.

One of the most successful art museums of the 1960s was the Louisiana Mu-seum of Modern Art, located just north of Copenhagen. It was originally an entirely private initiative of the publisher and businessman Knud W. Jensen, and for its first two decades ran without public subsidy. Jensen felt Denmark lacked a museum of international modern art, and he decided to do some-thing about it. He bought a villa in 1958, not to live in but to fill with art. Anyone interested could take the key from under the doormat, and let themselves in. He wanted people to feel at home with art. In this he was fol-lowing in a fine Danish tradition of private individuals making entirely pub-lic gestures. His most famous precursor was Carl Jacobsen, the brewer who spent all of his spare time and fortune creating his great public art gallery, the Glyptotek in Copenhagen (now the Ny Carlsberg Glyptotek). Jacobsen did not want to call it a 'museum' because he thought this implied too analytical and cold an approach. He wanted his art to be 'displayed in festivity and har-mony, to grace the life of the living'. He said at its opening in 1906, 'by all means let the Winter Gardens attract people to the Glyptotek … when they see the palms this may prompt them to think about the sculptures'.

Jacobsen and Jensen wanted to show art in a domestic setting but, unlike other wealthy collectors of their times like Frick and Burrell, in domestic settings designed for the public, not for private individuals. To create an am-bience in which people could be at ease looking at art, Jensen extended the house he had bought and, over the years, established Louisiana as one of the most famous and most original modern art museums in the world. It set a new standard of gallery design for the post-war period even though it was not a new building but an extension of a modest family home, set in a beautiful garden overlooking the sea. The main entrance is the front porch and visitors first of all find themselves in a living room filled with art. The impression that they get is that they are going to enjoy a purely domestic experience. However, they soon find themselves drawn along glazed corridors that lead them through the garden, with views of sculptures by Joan Miró, Henry Moore and Alexander Calder placed among the trees, on the lawns or overlooking the sea. The corridors themselves lead to a domino sequence of full-sized, purpose-built galleries containing an array of masterpieces of post-war European and American art. At every junction between the gallery spaces, visitors are given glimpses of the surrounding landscape and are encouraged to walk out and contemplate the many works of art arranged throughout the garden. When they do so it is as though the garden is everything; the galleries themselves are cleverly hidden behind the trees or sunk into the rolling lawns and flowerbeds. Art and nature are here in harmony. The museum expresses the clear aesthetic that art provides an imaginative, contemplative experience, and goes on to assert, by implication, that the measure of human nature is nature itself. There are two spaces in this museum: the internal spaces in the galleries and the space outside. The gallery itself has no exterior; it does not face the world. You enter it or leave it as you would your own home. That is the place, this gallery claims, of art in our lives. It is a wonderfully confident and comforting assertion. But can it be sustained when so much art no longer celebrates harmony with nature but warns of our abuse of it?

Nothing could be further from the modest front door that leads you into Louisiana, than the towering blank walls of Tate Modern's converted power station, yet they are both galleries of modern art. Neither can, nor would, disclaim the first impression they make on their visitors. One implies that art is humane and accessible; the other that art is elemental and powerful. Art at its best is neither one nor the other but both. The problem with conversions is that the museum is stuck with the appearance they have inherited, instead of creating one of their own. Britain has been waiting for a national gallery of modern art for a long time. Every director of the Tate, since the Second World War, has tried to untangle the Duchamps and Picassos from the Hogarths and Constables. The Lottery has at last provided the funds to do it. The options the Tate faced were to build anew on a prime vacant site on the South Bank, next to the Festival Hall, or to convert a partially disused power station further down river. Money was not at issue. It cost nearly twice as much to convert the power station into Tate Modern as it did to build Frank Gehry's gleaming new Guggenheim in Bilbao. This decision will, perhaps, in time, come to be seen as the manifestation of a lack of faith, on the Tate's part, in the role of art in contemporary society, and in the ability of contemporary architects to express this. If so, it will be seen as just another instance of a more widespread failure – the lack of confidence museums feel in telling the world what they are really about. The Tate could have proved that it was possible to build a modern museum that would attract people in as well as serve the needs of its collection and, in the process, help to create an icon for the role of modern art in society today. This would have been an exciting challenge, especially given the exuberance of contemporary architecture – an art form to which the British have made an outstanding contribution and one that surely merits celebration in their new national gallery of modern art.

In the Far East, where the few old buildings that do exist, such as temples, have been preserved only because they remain in use, museums have had to be given new premises. During the boom years in the 1970s and 1980s, every major city in Japan built a new museum of art. There are over 20 of them, all different, but all somehow oddly the same. Local architects have been used in nearly every case, and their brief seems to have been to produce a building that is at once imposing and anonymous. The resulting concrete blocks in varying configurations of geometric forms, all inhuman in scale, celebrate the economic prosperity of a region, rather than what they contain. Often this is precious little. Though fully air-conditioned and equipped with the latest display systems, these galleries contain minute collections filling only a fraction of their massive storage areas and, as one curator told me, they have very little money to acquire things, show exhibitions or, in many cases, even open their doors to let the public in. The most successful art galleries in Japan are those that are incorporated into other organisations. One of the most impressive I have seen was run in the extensive basements of a new Buddhist temple, as part of its educational programme. Another favourite option is to incorporate a museum into a department store, usually on the top floor. The idea is to attract the customers in to see the exhibits and then have them leave through all the tempting merchandise on the lower floors; a new concept in cascade selling. Many museum curators in the West are rather horrified by this juxtaposition of commerce and culture and only the superb technical standards of these department-store museums and, it has to be admitted, the offer of cash, induces them to lend their collections to these venues.

The penetration of the museum into the marketplace could, however, offer stimulating possibilities for museums, if it proves possible to establish a creative encounter between museums and shopping, one in which people planning to buy something would be able to see a display showing what would have been available to them in the past, at what comparative price and of what range of quality according to their purse and class. Then they would be able to assess the relative merits of what was on offer to them today. The past, then, could be a stimulator to the present, not just by educating the critical judgment of the consumer but also by challenging the aspirations of the maker. A pilot scheme ran along just these lines by Glasgow Museums in a Habitat store failed in the end because of the difficulty of marrying the management methods of the retail and museum worlds. They operate at totally different speeds; 12 months is years away in the retail business, but it is tomorrow for museums. To make a future version of the project work would require a major commitment on the part of both the museum and the shop involved. It is worth a try, because all the teapots and tables, clothes and cars in museums were originally made for sale, just like merchandise today, and they could therefore be used to stimulate more thought about manufacture and merchandise today. It would be a perfect project for the V&A, but to achieve such a marriage would require shopkeepers to sacrifice selling-space for contemplation, while curators would need to learn how to work much more rapidly and spontaneously, literally in the marketplace.

The correspondence between shopping and museums has been observed before. Karl Moritz, the German philosopher, when walking down the Strand in 1782 (then London's main shopping street), likened the large and well-lit shop windows selling 'every production of art and industry' to 'a well-regulated cabinet of curiosities'. Today, shopping and museum visiting are both family, daytime, all-weather activities with some eating and drinking, a lot of looking and some buying. Increasingly, too, shops combine cultural experiences, like the art galleries that are now a common feature of furniture and bookstores. Since shopping is the most popular leisure activity today, it would do a great deal to increase the amount of exposure of works of art to the public, if museums could make a meaningful marriage with merchandising.

Something of the atmosphere that it could be possible to create can be sensed at the 1853 Gallery in Salts Mill, near Bradford, in the north of England, where there is a gallery combined with an art shop, fashion house, restaurant and performance space. It was created by Jonathan Silver, a Bradford textile and clothes merchant who was passionately interested in art. Whenever I have been there, the place has been packed with people enjoying themselves. There is no artificial distinction, there, between looking at books in the shop, or pictures in the gallery, drinking coffee or listening to music. These are all activities that the handsome interior spaces of the old mill amply contain. Visitors feel totally at ease, alive and responsive; they do not have to be art lovers or art experts, they can be themselves and therefore feel confident in their response. Salts Mill does have one unique asset, however, which helps it achieve its goals. Jonathan Silver was a close friend of the Bradford-born artist, David Hockney, whose work is naturally outgoing, bright and inclusive, and his pictures contribute a great deal to the egalitarian spirit of this exceptional art gallery.

Can a museum be in a shopping centre? The answer has to be yes. A museum only requires two elements – people and things, not walls and a roof. A museum without people is not a museum but a store. A museum without things is not a museum but a theme park. A museum can happen in an imposing environment specially built for the purpose, like the British Museum, or in a multi-purpose hall like the Exploratorium in San Francisco, or in a church, a castle, a shopping centre, in the street, at home, in a van, on a train or, as happens in Sweden, on a ship. There could be a museum in every school in Britain, not just in Eton and Harrow. Sir Henry Cole understood this when he started the South Kensington Museum's Circulation Departments, which toured wonderful things around the country until they were closed, by the V&A in 1978, and by the Science Museum, having been devolved to Newcastle Museums, in 1989. The Open Museum, founded in Glasgow in 1990, aimed at reaching out to new audiences in a new way. It started with what people were interested in and where they were, not with what the museum was interested in and where it was. So people were invited into Glasgow Museums' stores to select what captivated them and then, with the help of the Open Museum staff, they borrowed these items and created their own exhibition in their own community. I remember vividly the opening of an exhibition about men's exploitation of women told through the history of clothing, put on by a women's group in a community centre in Easterhouse, one of the most deprived peripheral housing schemes in Glasgow. The occasion was serious, hilarious and packed. Nobody could say that this corner of a community hall was not for that fortnight a museum, and the most genuinely accessible I have ever known. Museums do not need buildings to work, but if they have one, or build one, they need to make sure it attracts people in, and does not put them off.

The Pompidou Centre, Paris

One of the few modern buildings to present a new, external image of the museum in our times is the Pompidou Centre in Paris, though it has to be remembered it is a library and cultural centre as well. The Pompidou has been extremely successful in welcoming people in: 150 million people have been through its doors since it opened in 1977, attracted initially to the great piazza in front of it, to gaze up at its multi-coloured facade. They then get drawn down the slope and find themselves being sucked into one of its unprepossessing doors, only to be carried up the escalators to enjoy the sight of Paris falling away beneath them, with a wonderful view opening up across the rooftops to the Eiffel Tower to the west and Montmartre to the north.

This building, however, is still essentially built from the outside in, quite literally in fact, because all the guts and organs of the building decorate the exterior. The inside consists of nothing more than layer upon layer of empty, open spaces that have to be adapted to service exhibitions. The works of art in them look drab and dreary rather than bright and lively, due to the temporary screens, the artificial lighting and the oppressive ceiling heavily loaded with industrial pipes and conduits, though marginal attempts have been made to rectify this during the recent overhaul. The only shows I saw that looked good in the original space were the remarkable exhibitions about the cultural exchange between Paris and Berlin and Moscow, curated by Pontus Hulton. These worked because they were not only about art in its purest aesthetic context, but also about art in its relationship to cultural expression as a whole. Paintings by Matisse were hung next to stills from films and architectural models. The whole kaleidoscope chimed naturally with the buildings' exposed technology and marketplace atmosphere. Usually when a curator at the Pompidou Centre wants to create an environment suitable to the works on show, he or she can only do so by building walls and ceilings that obliterate the container. The permanent displays in the Pompidou Centre may not look as good as they could, but the building does face the world with open arms. It is a step towards a cathedral for culture in our times, even if its interior is still soulless.

One of the most famous museum buildings of recent years is I.M. Pei's pyramid at the Louvre. It is a daring structure in the centre of the great forecourt of the Palace. Everyone is drawn towards it and down into the vast subterranean space beneath. But they are not then entering the museum. This famous building is not a museum at all but a cap for a concourse area and an upmarket shopping mall. The British Museum's new Great Court, designed by Foster and Partners and opened in 2000, is still, essentially, only a concourse. It provides London with a magnificent new, covered public space, but it is also important for the museum. The Great Court has the effect of opening up the museum's heart, though the staff have yet to find a way of carrying its egalitarian spirit into the body of the museum. If museums are the cathedrals of our times, their architects have only so far built the naves and spires, hardly ever an apse. There is one, and a cloister too, in Daniel Libeskind's new Jewish Museum in Berlin, although these have not been built for the contemplation of exhibits, but purely for architectural expression.

The new Jewish Museum in Berlin was commissioned in 1989 as an extension of the Berlin Museum, which tells the history of the city, concentrating particularly on the 20th Century. It includes in its collection portraits of Hitler and Goering. The extension, which was completed in 1998, dwarfs the modest classical building that gave it birth, and which still provides it with its entrance. The Jewish Museum, as it has come to be known, has no front door of its own. Libeskind was adamant about this. He wanted Jewish history to be seen within the context of German history; his concept for the extension is that it manifests a hidden story. His building rises sheer out of the ground like a monumental, metal-clad cliff face, zig-zagging into the distance. You can walk all around it but you cannot walk into it, for the link that connects it to the Berlin Museum is a hidden subterranean passageway. There are no windows, either, at ground level to give you a welcoming glimpse into the interior, or an opportunity for those inside to look out. The whole effect is of an armour-plated prison, and one in which torture is practised, for what windows there are, are high up and set at angles that lacerate the sheer metal sides like wounds. This is certainly a museum that attempts to express what it is about. But there was immediately a dispute about the message the building projected when it was finished. More people might have found it acceptable if the museum had been solely about the history of anti-Semitism in Germany, but it was supposed to be a celebration of Jewish life and its contribution to society as well. As the architect Izi Metzstein expressed it: 'if they want to round us up again, that's where they'll put us'.

The building's interior is as dramatic as its exterior. You enter it through a gash in the wall and floor of one of the classical interiors in the Berlin Museum, and descend a steep staircase into a dark, angular pit, feeling that you are about to enter the set of an early German Expressionist horror movie, such as *Nosferatu* or *The Cabinet of Dr Caligari*. When you reach the bottom, a long tunnel extends before you, its length dramatically emphasised by a streak of fluorescent light that runs along the centre of its black roof. A label tells you where you are and what to think:

> You are now underground. Ahead of you is the Axis of Continuity. This leads to the stairs that take you to the main exhibition. The Axis of Exile and the Axis of the Holocaust cut across your path and

lead to the Garden of Exile and the Holocaust Tower. Architect Daniel Libeskind asks us to think about the Holocaust and those people deported to their deaths; Exile and those able to escape; and Continuity – those who live on.

It is tempting, at this stage, to explore the Axis of the Holocaust or Exile, instead of going straight ahead along the Axis of Continuity, if only because the latter leads to a flight of stairs three times as high as the one you have just walked down. But one of the interpretation staff, and this museum has many, seeing me hesitate, encouraged me to see the exhibition first because, she said, the displays are demanding, and best done when I am fresh, while this part of the museum, she added, indicating the corridors around her, is the emotional part. She was right. The building *is* in two distinct parts: first there are the underground passageways leading to the architectural/sculptural expressions of the Garden of Exile and the Holocaust Tower; second, there are the exhibition galleries that occupy two, quite narrow floors between the angular zig-zagging walls of the main building. Even when they were empty these spaces were visually hectic, because of their angular vistas, sudden bends and the slanting rays of light falling across from the random gashes of windows. They were designed without any specific exhibits in mind.

It was hardly surprising, therefore, that when the extension was built, no one quite knew what to do with it: should it tell the story of the Holocaust, or the history of the Jews in Berlin, or, as many suggested, should it be left empty as a monumental piece of Expressionist, environmental sculpture? While the debate raged, the public were able to visit the whole building, empty. From the beginning of 1999 to the end of 2000, it attracted no fewer than 350,000 visitors. But something had to be done with all those empty exhibition corridors, and eventually it was decided to install a display that would tell the whole history of the Jews in Germany from Roman times until today. The installation, created at breakneck speed in 18 months, was masterminded by Ken Gorbey, who had made his reputation with his displays at Te Papa Tangarewa, the new national museum of New Zealand, which opened in 1998 using a mixture of interactive, video and computer technology alongside conventional exhibits, to create an educational entertainment for the whole family, a formula that proved immensely popular. But the subject of the Jewish museum and the linear configurations of the galleries militate against this pick-and-choose approach. The playground areas (one with rocking horses, used to inculcate military values in children's minds in the 18th and 19th centuries, or so we are told), jammed into

Libeskind's uncomfortable corners, and the occasional crawl-through tunnels, floored with cushions, the entrance marked 'only for kids' (one near a display on the 1873 Stock Market collapse), look out of place and unloved in this installation and are unlikely to be used.

More seriously, the installation team decided to tell their visitors, in stages, what being a Jew means. So, quite early in the exhibition one comes across a joyous book illustration (sadly only a photographic reproduction) dated 1310–30, showing Jewish children on their first day at school, each receiving a letter baked in dough, to demonstrate to them that learning can be sweet. We are informed that all Jewish children, both boys and girls, were taught to read (unlike Christian children at that time) so that they would be able to read the scriptures for themselves (unlike Christian adults at that time) – a practice that greatly influenced Martin Luther and the whole development of Christianity, especially in Germany. So much more could have been made of this exhibit if it had not been buried in the general mêlée, and it would have been even more memorable if the original volume (in the State Library in Berlin) had been on display. Later on in the exhibition, we come to an obscure engraving illustrating the practice of ritual bathing after menstruation, accompanied by a label with a footnote which tells us that, 'by the way, the Christian tradition of baptism has its origins in this Jewish tradition' (an interpretation that would surprised John the Baptist). But it is not until we get to the 19th century that we are told about the major rituals of britmila, bar mitzvah and, even, Shabbat. Looking at a circumcision bench of 1766, we learn about the importance of this ceremony, when the newborn son is named and becomes a child of Israel. The word 'bench' is a misnomer for this exhibit. It is one of the most remarkable in the whole museum – a splendid, baroque carved settee, upholstered in red damask, emblazoned with religious texts that surround a magnificent imperial eagle, embossed in gold – the whole ensemble a telling symbol of the ability and desire of Jewish people to be assimilated into the society in which they live, while keeping their own traditions alive. This unique survival could have been used to bring this crucial point vividly to life, had the whole issue of circumcision been dealt with at the beginning, as would have been more fitting.

If visitors were given an understanding of what it means to be Jewish right at the start of the display, then everything later would have fallen into place. As it is, the first exhibit you see, as you turn off the staircase that concludes the Axis of Continuity, is a photograph of a sculpture of the Emperor Constantine, above a panel that tells you: 'Constantine introduced Christianity as a state religion, which made things worse for the Jews in the long run'. If one has no grasp of the relationship of Judaism to Christianity (and one cannot assume this among the majority of visitors), one cannot hope to begin to understand, for example, the significance of the saccharine 18th-century painting included in the display, which shows the boy St Werner of Oberwesel, whom Christians believed was murdered by Jews to provide them with the human blood they needed for their religious ceremonies, nor can one begin to understand the waves of anti-Semitism that swept through Europe, particularly when times were hard, let alone during the Holocaust. The latter is dealt with in a surprisingly perfunctory way in this museum, indicated by a few personal possessions of victims displayed in white showcases behind white gauze hangings that attempt to soften the severity of the architecture and subdue the ever-present, lacerating rays of light.

There is one point in the story, however, when the containing architecture does chime well with the display. This is the section dealing with the early 20th century, when Jews enjoyed legal and, to a certain extent, social equality, and a period that saw the opening of Berlin's first Jewish Museum in 1933 (it was closed in 1938). This era saw Jewish people making brilliant contributions to science, commerce and the arts. It is a time that Daniel Libeskind feels most at home in, and the point where he personally picks up the Axis of Continuity. The expressiveness of the images from those times, in paintings, buildings, posters and films, chimes with Libeskind's shooting galleries and exploding light. For the first time in this museum one feels that one is in a harmonious space. But this is a chance marriage of form and content; it was not intended. All Libeskind's creativity and passion has gone into the architectural prelude to the museum, the Axis leading to the Holocaust Tower, where you find yourself at the bottom of a vast, hollow, concrete pit lit only by one narrow slit of light way above your reach, or the Axis that leads to the Garden of Exile, a disorientating, sunken open space, with a sloping, cobbled floor, congested with leaning concrete pillars topped, far above your head, with flourishing willow trees. Had Daniel Libeskind developed his building with the curators who were compiling the story, and not used the commission solely as an opportunity for personal expression, he could have created with them a brilliant, intellectual and dramatically moving museum, that would have told the whole joyous and horrific story of the Jews in Germany, both through exhibits and through architecture. As it is, the museum in the Jewish Museum is merely a side-show.

The same cannot be said for the Vasa Museum in Stockholm, designed by Marianne Dählbuck and Görån Mansson, and opened in 1990. When first seen across the harbour, you immediately ask yourself 'What's that?' The building looks like a pile of sheds that have grown on their own, out of which protrude the masts of a ship – or like a tempestuous wave that, on the point of engulfing a wreck, has itself been turned to wood. You cannot keep your eyes off it as you are drawn towards it across the bay, not because it is flashy, but because it is so intriguing. Only when you go inside do you realise that the exterior is entirely logical; it simply encases the walkways and interpretation bays that take the visitors around the ship that is this museum's main exhibit. By letting its function inspire its form, this museum is as beautiful as a Romanesque cathedral.

The copper domes of the Canadian Museum of Civilization, Hull, Quebec, signal internal spaces, but the sweeping terraces do not take their form so much from the galleries inside, being instead symbolic of the Canadian landscape. The architect Douglas Cardinal wanted to give an impression of Canada at the end of the ice age when man first settled there and, by doing so, emphasise the point that Canadian civilisation is founded on mankind's relationship with nature. The flowing walls of fossil-studded Manitoba limestone are unforgettably evocative, but the theme is not carried through the internal displays, as it could have been to great effect. The internal and external visions are not in harmony.

The Groninger Museum located at the northern tip of the Netherlands and opened in 1994, is another example of a museum that has tried to make its purpose naked. It is the product of a creative collaboration between a curator, a designer and a city council. First of all they thought of their public. The Council wanted the museum to incorporate a new footbridge across the canal that would link the city centre with the railway station. The Museum welcomed this with open arms. Such a site, on the canal, opened up many imaginative possibilities as well as guaranteeing that vast numbers of people would see, pass by and, it was hoped, enter the new museum. The collection contains old masters, decorative arts, archaeology and contemporary arts, and it was decided at an early stage to use this diversity as a starting point. The brilliant Italian designer and artistic jack-of-all-trades, Alessandro Mendini, was approached to provide a master plan and commission other architects and designers to create a sequence of distinctly different pavilions in the water on each side of the bridge, to contain the different aspects of the collections. Variety was to be the key, not conformity. There would be no uniform white walls or polished wooden floors, no conforming aesthetic. In this museum, each space was to have its own personality. The underlying principle was that everyone and everything is different, and that strengthening the individual personality of a space strengthens the personality of what it contains, and how it presents itself to the world.

The pavilion designed by Philippe Starck and Albert Geertjes provides a soft white, curved space, hung with flowing curtains, an admirable setting for the museum's decorative arts and unique Chinese porcelain collection, which was salvaged from a wreck in 1986 and displayed here, again in the water under the visitors' feet. And the old masters look good hung in the pavilion by Coop Himmelb(l)au, which looks as though Piranesi had built it with iron girders. And the visitors love it; they come alive in these spaces. There is no hushed reverence here; people feel free to express their own views, as the designers and artist have expressed theirs. The embracing confidence of this gallery springs in part from the personality of its director, Frans Haks. He is an exhibit in his own museum. The photographer Inez van Lamsweerde has portrayed him standing in the golden mosaic archway of Mendini's showroom in Milan. His silver hair is brushed back from his smooth forehead and his dark navy silk jacket is parted to reveal his blue and gold floral damask waistcoat. He beams at us through his glasses with a defiant smile fixed across his lips. In a way his personality is the personality of the museum and that is its strength. He is a curator of modern art who does not hide his personal judgment behind a veil of dubious objectivity.

It is easy to criticise the Groninger Museum. It has suffered two major floods and after five years is undergoing a major refit. But it has given a great deal of enjoyment and interest to a great number of people who would not have gone to a more conventional, less strategically sited gallery. The only serious criticism I have is that its tower is not real gold. It was a brilliant concept to build a storage room as a golden Egyptian obelisk rising into the sky, to contain all Groninger's artistic treasures. But sadly this tower, even in sunlight, struggles to become a muddy yellow. This creates an appropriately Postmodern clash with the green algae that now grows in the water at its base, but it is not the symbol that Groninger or its museum needs. The best thing would be to gild this tower properly. Then it could point the way forward to a golden future for symbolic museum building, worldwide.

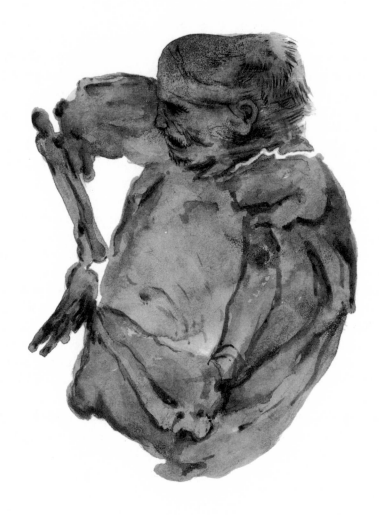

Lindow Man, the body of a 25-year-old man who had been stunned, garrotted and then bled to death, found preserved in a bog near Manchester in 1985, *c*.500 CE.
British Museum

CHAPTER TEN

The Poetic Museum

So what will poetic museums be like in the future? There are many indica-
tors among museums today. The United States Holocaust Memorial Museum in Washington must surely be the best museum in the world, if you judge
a museum not by what it contains but by what it gives its visitors. As many as
5,000 people continue to pour through this museum every day, and being with
them is an experience one does not forget. I have never been in a crowd so attentive, so silent, so moved and so slow moving. No one 'does' this museum in
less than about three hours. The pacing of the display is immaculate; your attention is held at each point, yet nothing is skimped, and unlike most museum
displays, visitors feel impelled to see everything and read everything, not because they feel they have to but because they want to. Hurrying in this museum becomes pointless, and increasingly, as one goes round, disrespectful.

The United States Holocaust Memorial Museum

The architecture of the United States Holocaust Memorial Museum in
Washington, designed by James Ingo Freed of Pei, Cobb and Freed, is
highly successful at conveying a mood the moment you enter. It does
not do this by using images of suffering, but purely through abstract
means. You sense at once that you are not in a comforting, human environment, but a vast uncomfortable space, with metal gantries high up in
the rafters. It is like entering a factory in which you soon discover that it
is you yourself who is on the production line. None of this is stated; it is
all a question of feeling. It works emotionally on you and prepares you
for what is to come. This is very fine architecture in the service of a museum, though we are only talking about the interior space; the exterior is
just another bland block in the capital.

The museum itself, the contents of this building, is Jeshajahu
Weinberg's masterpiece (sadly he died before he could realise his dream
to create a museum that told the life of Jesus and the birth of Christianity). To tell the story of the Holocaust he drew on all the narrative skills he
had developed at the Museum of the Jewish Diaspora in Tel Aviv and the
Museum of the History of Jerusalem in the Tower of David in Israel, but
with one important difference: for the first time he used real objects, and

essentially only real objects. The huge team who worked on the project scoured the world for material evidence of the Holocaust. Their efforts were rewarded, and proved justified when 'Holocaust Denial' reared its ugly head. The story is told almost entirely through the means of contemporary documentation, photographs, film clips, books, posters, propaganda material, records, letters and other archival material, interspersed with real artefacts, which the organisers found to be the most telling. Few things bring the horror more vividly to life than the personal possessions – suitcases, hairbrushes, shoes – taken from the victims as they entered the gas chambers. The presentation is conventional; there are introductory panels and every item is labelled, in white on black, to explain why it is worth looking at. A conscious decision was made not to use sound (there is sound in the bays showing films and playing audio tape, but these are insulated from the main thoroughfare). The silence among the visitors increases as the story unfolds, until it becomes a palpable part of the experience, all the more so as the evidence accumulates to show how a conspiracy of silence let this happen.

In a very few instances models are used, particularly of things that could not be moved, such as an immaculate cast of a remaining section of the Warsaw ghetto wall, a shoddy but effective construction; or another, again true to scale, of the sign that hung over the entrance to the Auschwitz death camp, '*Arbeit Macht Frei*' (Work Brings Freedom). The most remarkable model, however, is a recreation by the Polish sculptor, Jan Stobierski, of an earlier model he made for the museum at Auschwitz, showing how people were killed in the gas chambers. Visitors start on the top floor of the Holocaust Museum (it is the reverse at the Museum of the Jewish Diaspora) and are led slowly down, and down, to this unforgettable sight – a crowd of people, clearly bewildered, being led, through a sequence of underground chambers, to their death, all individually carved, and broadly personalised, and all painted white. This 'model' must rank as one of the great sculptures of the second half of the 20th century. A museum of the Holocaust without the gas chambers is unthinkable, but how can one represent them? Art alone can provide the means. This is a museum not just of facts but of feelings – it incorporates a Hall of Remembrance at the end, in which visitors can light candles in memory of the departed – and, as such, heralds a new age for museums.

One of the best modern narrative museums is the Vasa Museum in Stock-holm. It has become the most popular museum in Sweden because it tells its story so well, but it does have a remarkable object at its centre. The Vasa was the greatest flagship of the 17th century, but it only managed to sail a few hundred yards out into Stockholm harbour before it keeled over and sank with all crew on board, right in front of a crowd assembled to see its maiden voyage. It lay there for centuries, stripped of its paintwork, but preserved in every other detail in the brackish waters of the delta. It has now been raised and is on display in a museum in a dry dock in the harbour. Standing under its prow and looking up at its massive timber sides, carved with gargoyles and fantastic figures and decorations, with a roaring lion's head at each gun por-tal to scare the enemy, gives one a vivid impression of the scale, danger and pageantry of war at that time – and the craftsmanship and inventiveness within the extremely restricted technology of woodwork and rigging. The sight of this ship is one of the wonders of the world. Nothing I know brings the 17th century so much to life, in one amazing eyeful. And its story is en-hanced by the museum, which takes you on a journey up six levels of walk-ways around the ship, telling you all about its construction, its purpose and its crew (whose possessions were miraculously preserved too, knives and blankets, hats and jackets neatly packed in preparation for the voyage). In a bay near the end, you can sit in a reconstructed courtroom and listen in your chosen language to the trial that was held to identify the culprits who had caused the disaster, and which had to be abandoned when it became evident that the king himself was to blame for demanding too big a vessel.

The Holocaust Museum in Washington and the Vasa Museum in Stock-holm both have the advantage of dealing with one subject in depth. They have fixed displays that lead their visitors on set journeys of discovery. This is not the case for most museums, which have many and changing stories to tell. If museums in general are going to develop narrative displays they will have to find a way of doing so that allows for adaptation and change. The Holocaust Museum itself suffers from this lack of flexibility; occasionally items are removed for conservation, research or loan and not replaced, and the visitor's experience is interrupted in ways that are inconsistent with its serious purpose. The Neanderthal Museum in Germany, another brilliant narrative museum which tells one story – of the discovery and significance of the hominid remains found in the quarry where the museum is now sit-ed – highlights the problems that can arise when a museum creates a 'permanent' installation. None of the scientific advisers to the Neanderthal Museum could have imagined that within a year of its opening, traces of DNA would be discovered in Neanderthal bones. Some specialists maintain that this DNA might have deteriorated so much as to make any conclusions drawn from its analysis invalid. Whoever was right, the museum had at least to find a way, which it had not budgeted for, of making the displays address the new evidence. It would be much better, however, if the Neanderthal Museum had not just responded passively after the event, but had been so designed and managed that it could be at the forefront of the debate, presenting the issues to the public in new displays, and thereby generating more interest in its subject. Capacity for change needs to be inherent in museum displays. Once it is, they will not only be able to keep abreast of contemporary issues but also deal with many different subjects at once. Then dramatic and poetic presentations will not be restricted to one-subject museums in permanent displays, but will spread through the whole museum world.

We began by looking at the origin and subsequent development (shrinkage might be a better word) of the British Museum, the mother of all modern museums. How can this museum be changed so that all its exhibits become eloquent? The British Museum has the resources to respond to a whole host of contemporary issues. An issue in the news or the subject of a conference, a new archaeological discovery or a request by the public could provoke a display. Small displays could change continuously, breathing new meaning throughout the collection. There could be one, today, on Nebuchadnezzar, for example. This Biblical figure may seem as distant as you can get from contemporary concerns, until one learns that one of Saddam Hussein's propaganda tactics is to model himself on that despotic king. Saddam appears on handsome posters, dressed in a reconstructed costume of that period, to demonstrate the longevity of his culture. His attempt to recreate the Hanging Gardens of Babylon is similarly motivated. Or the museum might display, on the fifth day of the fifth month of the lunar calendar, a statue of Chu Yuan, not to admire its place in the history of Chinese art, but to ponder on the nature of a society that still celebrates the death, every year, of a poet of the 3rd century BCE who took his own life because he failed to persuade the Emperor to improve the lot of the people. As China gains in global importance, one role of the British Museum could be to deepen our understanding of its culture.

The British Museum has a huge canvas; it can introduce a vast public to all the great civilisations of the world. It does not have to do this by mounting theme-park displays presenting dramatised generalisations about life in Ancient Egypt or Greece, or by using its collections to illustrate a compendium of information that would be more usefully and accessibly presented as a computer programme or in a book. The great advantage museums have is that the objects in their collections can carry so much of a display's meaning. Museums can use the wonderful things in their collections to open windows directly onto fascinating worlds. An Egyptian papyrus boat, an Aztec golden raft and a Viking ship were all used to convey the dead into the next world. Imaginatively displayed, objects like these, though so far removed from our own lives, could evoke profound feelings in the visitor so as to prevent any trivialisation of the subject, such as the superficial reactions inspired by cadavers or mummies. It is perfectly possible for a museum to communicate genuine religious belief, and avoid the pitfalls of conflicting doctrines, by allowing faiths to be expressed through the works of art that were created for them and the personal testimonies of believers, where these are still practised, or by personal historical accounts where not – this methodology was used to great effect in the St Mungo Museum of Religious Life and Art in Glasgow. By such means, the British Museum could mount revelatory displays about the great religions of the world (ideally treating Judaism, Christianity and Islam as one family), as well as exploring the nature of religion itself and the common themes that many share, such as the conflict between an active and contemplative life, a recurring subject in so much religious art, from Christian Europe to Buddhist China. 'To be or not to be' is an ideal theme for a museum because it has been dealt with so profoundly, and entertainingly, by a myriad of artists and craftsmen in the past.

At its core, the British Museum would still need to mount displays about the great civilisations that have shaped our world. Few museums are better placed, for example, to introduce a wide audience to the civilisation of the Ancient Greeks. Such a display would need to tell the story of everyday life, of food and wine, sex and death, sport, politics and drama, and several raucous gods, not separated, as such displays are now on different floors within the museum, but integrated so that one can look from pots to sculptures, coins to texts with a rising crescendo of understanding. The collections are so rich that, with the careful juxtaposition of objects and the judicious use of reconstructions, visitors could piece together their own picture of, say, the small community of Athens building its marble vision of mental order on a towering rock, surrounded by a ring of mountains and the sea, and what was to them a barbaric world beyond. No display about the Greeks makes sense unless it deals with the subsequent influence of Greek thought upon the world, their concept of democracy and the nobility of man. Why should we in the West always separate, for example, the works of the Renaissance from the classical culture that gave it birth? People need to be shown that there have been not just one but several renaissances since (and including) Roman times, demonstrating the power that Greek thought has continued to exert over our minds, through the so-called Dark Ages right up until the present. It would be perfectly possible to design a display that enables visitors to appreciate something of this history of thought as they look at a statue of a Greek athlete; that is, in addition to learning to identify the phases of classical art. The only difference between such displays and what is seen at present would be a matter of emphasis. The exhibits would be the same, but the interpretation would be different, affecting, if necessary, their installation. Statues of athletes, for example, were not created to face us, but to face the gods. They were positioned as permanent suppliants before altars, representing an individual's petition or thanks for a victory. Arrayed as they are, facing out from the walls of museums gives visitors quite the wrong impression; it makes us the gods. Rightly, we should first see their backs, and join with them in their salutations to the gods. Presentations in museums can helps us to glimpse the thoughts and feelings, hopes and fears of people in the past, and understand a little more about how they relate to us today.

Alongside central displays dealing with the great civilisations, religions and philosophies of the world, the British Museum could mount major displays dealing with crucial themes that permeate all societies, like health and sustenance, sex and power. Such themes only seem insurmountable when viewed in the abstract. When considered from the perspective of material evidence, they can be brought within everyone's reach. The British Museum is superbly well equipped to tackle a subject such as the history of the relationship between men and women. There could be a gallery full of goddesses and gods from all cultures and ages around the world, on whom many of our feelings and ideas about our sexuality have been projected. The sheer power, beauty and subtlety of so many of these images would ensure that such a subject was not reduced to a trite rendering of gender issues. It might even seem surprising to future generations, familiar with such a display, to learn that 20th-century London had three separate national museums dedicated to the Army, the Navy and to war in general, but no museum that threw light on the history of the relationship between the sexes. Increasing concerns about the environment could oblige the British Museum to mount a long-term display dealing with the history of mankind's relationship with other living creatures. Such a display would enable visitors to understand what the followers of Confucius meant when they claimed that water and fire have spirit but not life; that plants have spirit and life but not perception; that animals have all these but no sense of justice; and that it is only the latter which separates mankind from the beasts. Visitors may then begin to understand how crucially different this is from the Aristotelian view that has led people in the West to believe that man is separated from the animals solely by his capacity for rational, scientific thought, and to consider where that has got us.

The British Museum in the future could start by interesting its visitors in what is on show and lead them on from there. At present it uses its collections to illustrate broad themes, and as a result even the most wonderful things are often barely glanced at as visitors move from label to label. One of the British Museum's most famous exhibits is the Rosetta Stone. This rather nondescript slab is currently tucked in a corner of a gallery about Ancient Egypt, although its significance goes way beyond Egypt. It could easily serve as the centrepiece of a display that explores the origins of writing, not just that of Egypt and Greece, and not solely as a technical development, but as a device for communicating or withholding meaning. In *Mémoires d'Egypte*, a brilliant exhibition conceived by Hubert Bari for the National Library of France in 1990, visitors were able to relive the excitement of the discoveries of Jean François Champollion as they compared the Ancient Egyptian hieroglyphics with the other two scripts on the stone, the Egyptian cursive writing and the Greek text, both of which were translations. The visitors could then go on to hear, as if for the first time, the Book of the Dead and, as they were looking at an original papyrus, wonder how their own souls would weigh in the scales of justice against the feather of truth.

The British Museum could take the story of writing much further back, and then bring it right up to date. Every text in the display could be translated, on headsets, into each visitor's first language. Often ancient scripts like the cuneiform tablets from Mesopotamia, which look so strange to our eyes, actually describe the most mundane and familiar things, such as a dispute between neighbours or a schoolboy's exercise. Other texts could take one into very different worlds, full of weird gods pronouncing oracles and fortune-tellers interpreting dreams, which might well, after further consideration, not appear that far removed from our own times, either. Looking at hieroglyphs could lead you to Chinese calligraphy, to explore the origins of pictographs. The British Museum is fabulously rich in all this material. There could be many opportunities to attempt reconstructions of the sounds of ancient languages. Writing is usually divorced from speech in museums partly because museums to date have tended to collect signs rather than sounds. There is a vestige of cultural progressiveness in this; the invention or introduction of writing has usually been seen as a key indicator of civilisation, even though it is well known that societies as sophisticated as the Incas had no writing, and that many non-literate societies had an extremely rich oral tradition. The written word can be a diminution of the spoken one; much writing only comes fully alive when you hear it being spoken. Displays about writing need voices. Nobody leaving such a museum would think the past was silent, like a grave!

As currently arranged, the British Museum can never present more than a fraction at any one time of the fascinating themes its collection could inspire. There is a basic problem: many objects simply cannot be moved around with that much ease, and many, anyway, will be required for several different stories. But the great advantage visitors have over objects is that they *can* move. The British Museum's collection could be explored simultaneously, in countless directions, if the visitors, not the objects, followed the story line. Displays in the future could be designed to focus the visitor's attention on the objects, but interconnection between these objects would be in the visitor's minds. Though a great deal can be achieved simply by guiding people by means of hand-lists, a whole new world of possibilities opens with the development of personalised headsets.

The British Museum in future could be riddled with trails of interest running through it; these would be invisible, seen only by those following them as they listen to directions and interpretations on their headsets. Three different visitors could be looking at the *Lindow Man*, for example, at the same time, with three very different trains of thought in their minds. One could be fascinated by the neatly trimmed stubble on his cheek and suddenly feel the whole of Celtic Britain, which he had been learning about in the surrounding display, come vividly to life. Another could have just come from a display about divination, where she had been studying a model of a sheep's liver, marked with the physical blemishes to look out for immediately the organ had been plucked from the sacrificed beast. Her headset had guided her across the museum to the *Lindow Man*, whose death throes, as he entered the spirit world, might have been interpreted by those who sacrificed him as signs from the gods. At the same time, another visitor may be studying the brown leathery skin for traces of decoration. Though some experts think that the metallic pigments that have been found in *Lindow Man's* skin may have come from something he had eaten, many believe they are evidence of body paint. When his sacrificial body was thrown into the bog, *Lindow Man* could have been painted bright red and black, a brilliant green and an intense blue. The British Museum could mount the most wonderful trail through its collection about the colours of the past (the current fragment of a brightly coloured reconstruction in the Parthenon Galleries is deceptively crude). Scientists now have a much more accurate idea about the pigments and techniques that were used in painting in the past. A trail through the museum revealing their discoveries, using reconstructions and models, could come as a revelation to many visitors.

Sound could transform museum interpretation in the future. The beauty of sound is that you can listen and look at the same time, unlike labels, which distract one's attention. One of the best ways to visit a museum that contains unfamiliar material is to be taken round by a knowledgeable and enthusiastic curator. You are never likely to forget what you are taught to see for the first time. If a curator is not available, a sound guide is the next best thing, better than a tour guide, if it is well scripted and whispers in your ear what to look out for, lets you go round at your own pace and can be switched off at will. Soon every generation will be familiar with headsets, and the technology already exists to construct them so that there is no irritating noise spillage – this is essential for the museum environment, for there are few things more irritating than muffled buzzing, mumbling and thumping, when everything else is beautifully quiet.

One of the other frequently voiced objections to headsets is that they isolate people from one another. Museums are valued for the communal experiences they provide and many visitors like to share their experiences as they go round. Headsets need not be seen as a restriction on companionship or interaction, but as a way of extending and intensifying these. Headsets in the future could enable two or more people to share their experiences, interact with each other and learn together. Visitors will also soon be able to contact their friends in different parts of the museum, if they want to meet up or have found something especially interesting they want to share. It is only in their current, primitive state that headsets act more as an encumbrance than an aid to communication. Most usefully you can take them off, and then talk to your companion as loudly and enthusiastically as you please, without disturbing another visitor contemplating an icon in silence, or listening on his headset to the sound of monks chanting in an adjoining cloister. The headsets of the future could be very light and wire-less, and rest easily around one's shoulders, or slip into a pocket when not in use. Many people, used to perpetual background music, are put off by the hushed atmosphere other visitors find essential for their enjoyment. Some find music stimulates their awareness. Others prefer quiet study. All needs could be met in a museum wired for sound.

Headsets in the future could be programmed individually to receive the visitor's choice of language, or chosen package of information, pitched to suit the visitor's level of hearing. Headsets will also be able to send signals as well as receive them. They could tell a showcase, in which items have to be kept at a low light level for conservation reasons, to light up as a visitor approaches. Headsets, too, could send special signals for those with poor sight so that the illumination in the case can be increased. Special facilities like this could greatly increase the use of the museum by elderly people, who will, in

the future, constitute an increasingly large proportion of any museum's potential public. The majority of this generation are not being served at all in
the blanket gloom that pervades most galleries and museums. The museum
case of the future, too, could be intelligent, and be able to monitor the
amount of light exposure each object receives. It could record, too, how
many visitors look at it and for how long. If visitors regularly turn away at a
particular point, it may be that there is a fault in the storytelling. By this
means, unsuccessful displays could be earmarked for change or removal,
while much-used displays could be given an extended life. Headsets could be
designed so that the visitor can make choices as to how he or she goes
around the museum. They will be able to keep track of where you are, and
guide you to the café, for example, if you want a break, and then back to
where you were to continue your journey through the displays. Most valu-
ably, your personal headset will be able to talk to your computer after your
visit and record what you were most interested in, or at least what you spent
most time looking at (you could be surprised), and then let you know where
you can find out more about these subjects and see more examples in other
museums at home and abroad. In time this technology will enable you to explore the displays in advance on the museum's database, choose what you
want to see, and be taken to it when you arrive.

Let us imagine what a visit to the British Museum could be like in, say, 2012.
It is about ten o'clock at night. Jill, a 30-year-old computer programmer,
Jake, her 16-year-old nephew, Sophie, her 9-year-old niece, and their great-
uncle David are passing the British Museum on their way back from a show.
The last visitors are leaving and the guard is closing the gates. Sophie peers
through the railings and sees, amongst a group of statues standing in the otherwise eerily empty courtyard, a figure with a headdress full of birds' feathers
that looks like one of her favourite characters in the latest *Star Wars* trilogy.
Jill notices a poster about a show on the history of computer imaging, and
David spots that the entrance is free. He had last been to the museum over
50 years ago, he thinks, but the others have never visited before. On their
way home on the tube, they decide to make a visit the very next day, as it is
half-term. David needs a bit of persuading because his eyes are not as good as
they were and he fears he may not be able to see anything. Even the silent
Jake says he will come. He has nothing better to do.

The next day, Sophie's statue turns out to be a Highland Chief from Papua
New Guinea. His headdress is decorated with feathers taken from the tails of
birds of paradise. Jill wants her photograph taken standing next to a statue of

an Egyptian Priestess who has a beautiful, long face with high cheekbones and is almost unbelievably thin. She learns from the label that the priestess died over 3,000 years ago, that she led the chorus at the temple at Karnak and that her mummy can be seen within the museum. Jill's interest is already aroused.

A museum assistant smiles at them by the entrance at the top of the steps. He is dressed casually, not like a security guard, and wears a name badge. He is trained to spot first-time visitors, and can communicate simply in several languages. He explains how the museum works, where the cloakrooms, cafés and shops are, and encourages them to go into the Great Court, where they can choose what they want to see (because, he says, they will not be able to see everything in a day!) and buy headsets if they want because, as he explains, everything in the museum is wired for sound, and in almost all languages. He highly recommends the film show, Dr When, which gives the best introduction to the whole museum.

Encouraged, Jill, David and the two children walk on into the Great Court, with its vast, vaulted glass ceiling, through which they can see blue sky and scurrying clouds. There are several museum assistants demonstrating headsets. They confidently go up to one who is just saying goodbye, in Mandarin, to a group of Chinese visitors. Flags on her jumper indicate the languages she speaks. She explains that they can simply wander into the galleries to explore the museum by themselves, or go to one of the many computers around the perimeter of the Great Court to select what they want to see. She strongly advises them to buy headsets, which explain everything to them as they go around and in the language (or two) of their choice. David is intrigued: his mother used to speak to him in Yiddish, though he rarely uses the language now. He decides to go around with a bilingual set, because he is sure that doing so will trigger many memories. Sophie wants to try one out first to see if it is worth the expense. She slips a set on and walks up to a test case standing nearby. It contains a little blue sculpture of a hippopotamus. She jumps when she hears it bellow. A film sequence showing a hippo wallowing at a river's edge is projected onto the glass at the back of the case. She learns that the hippo is Opet, Goddess of Childbirth, and she was worshipped in Egypt over 40 lifetimes ago. Sophie is told that dates in the museum are given in terms of their number of human lives' away from us today, taking 70 years as an average. Conventional dates are given on the labels. Finally Sophie is told that she can see other animals in the museum, if she codes the 'animal tour' into her headset at the computer terminals.

All our party decide to buy headsets. David is particularly delighted with his because he can have them specially programmed to see the exhibits at higher light levels than normal. They can go off immediately and explore the galleries but, as the museum assistant explains, they would enjoy their visit much more if they find out how the museum works beforehand, by spending a minute or two at the computers. Once you have learnt how to use your headset, she explains, it will do most of the work for you, and guide you to what you want to see. They all go over to the computer desks, Jill and Jake taking one each and David sharing with Sophie. They learn that the museum is arranged chronologically over two floors, with the oldest material at the bottom and the more recent at the top. The ground floor deals with human origins and the emergence of the first great civilisations. The upper floor covers the period of the birth and spread of the world's largest religions, Judaism, Hinduism, Christianity, Islam, Sikhism and Buddhism and, with the emergence of modern science, finally brings the story up to date by showing the interaction of these religions with other ways of looking at the world. The exceptions to this are the thematic displays to the right of the Great Court, beginning with the King's Library, which shows the British Museum's first collections and what people did not know about the world in those times. Two adjacent galleries compare people's lives in the past to ours today, one showing how different their lives were, and another showing how extraordinarily similar they could be. Interspersed throughout the museum are thematic, comparative displays exploring the universal themes that bind all mankind together into one family.

Visitors are, however, discouraged from trying to see the whole museum in one go. Instead they are advised to start with something that interests them and to explore the museum from there. The museum displays are arranged as a constellation of stories, some small, some large, some linked, many separate. The larger ones take an hour or more to appreciate fully, others take half as long, and many can be enjoyed in ten minutes. Each of these displays tells a distinct story; each one like a window opening onto the past. All the displays are arranged in loosely chronological order, though some are thematic, comparing one age with another, and all of them are always being changed or updated in one way or another. There is no strict sequence to the displays; visitors can look at them in whatever order they wish. Something may catch their interest in one display that leads them directly to another part of the museum altogether. The guide on the headset points out these interconnections. Visitors can take a detour then, or go on as planned. Each visitor is encouraged to become an explorer. There are no right ways or wrong ways around the museum. Personal interest is the guiding principle.

Having chosen a 'young person's' headset, Sophie is not given a general introduction to the museum, but is asked immediately what she is interested in. She can answer by speaking into the computer's microphone. Images begin to rotate in front of her; there are cats and wigwams, Roman soldiers and pickaxes. A nod of her head indicates that she wants to sees something, or she can speak into the microphone if she has a special request. Sophie, who has a collection of lions of all shapes, sizes and substances in her bedroom, has no hesitation in stating clearly what she wants to see. Lions! Her headset says it will guide her to the lions in the museum. So off she goes, but David decides he had better follow to make sure she is all right.

Jake chooses the headset for grown-ups. A transparent three-dimensional projection of the whole museum appears in front of him on the screen, with a little red figure showing where he is sitting. The figure gets up and begins to take him on an introductory tour on the museum headset, but Jake becomes exhausted at the prospect of so many galleries. He realises that he can move the little figure himself about the museum and explore different spaces. In one gallery he discovers a full-scale model of the Quarkle Monster from the latest *Star Wars*. The computer tells him that the gallery takes you on a journey back in time, into the unknown and the realms of fear. He decides he would like to begin by seeing that, and he is about to set off, when his headset advises him to register his interests first, so that it can point out things of interest to him and advise him where to go next. A list of subjects begins to scroll down the screen. He is advised not to choose more than a couple because it could get confusing. He nods for 'football', and cannot resist doing the same for 'sex'. He then heads off across the Great Court to see his first display. As he walks away, listening to the directions, the voice on the headset asks him if he wants to hear some music as he goes round; rock, classical, world, pop, jazz or mood? One nod and he is listening to the latest disk by Bronze. He begins to quite like the place.

Jill skips through the menu on the computer screen to see what it has to offer. She quickly realises that she can connect through to the museum's main database and discover details about the vast array of collections in store, most of which are based at the museum's Study Centre across the road where, for a fee, she can make an appointment to see anything she wants. She notices that schools can explore the site and book directly, and that they, and community groups, can request certain items on loan! She must remember to tell her friend Jackie who runs a youth club about this. Since she has not been to the museum before, her headset strongly advises her to see the introductory film, Dr When, and to choose one or two other special interest features from the menu. She scrolls rapidly down the list, chooses 'Women' and 'Egypt', and goes down to the Film Theatre where, her headset tells her, the programme is about to start.

Dr When travels back in time in an old-fashioned red telephone box. The film begins with the world as it is today, spinning slowly around the sun. Aeroplanes fill the atmosphere, rockets take off for outer space, and the earth itself is covered with urban developments that glow golden in the shadow away from the sun's glare. Races of people are spread across the land, and stains of different hues show who controls whom, not just the power of countries but of companies. Large wild animals are isolated in tiny pockets. Then Dr When begins to go back in time, lifespan by lifespan. Slowly the numbers of people recede and the numbers of animals increase. The patterns of power change. The Europeans spread across the globe then retreat again. Columbus returns from America, as the Muslims return to Spain. After eight lifetimes, the world stops spinning around the sun and flattens out, and the continents move apart. Empires expand and contract, the Vikings, Charlemagne and the Holy Roman Empire, the Aztecs and the followers of Mohammed. The sun rises in the East and sinks in the West. The great civilisations grow up along the valleys of the Indus, the Yellow River, the Tigris and the Nile. The numbers of people get fewer and fewer and the earth, sea and air burgeon with creatures of every size, shape and hue. Eventually only specks of people are discernable sprinkled across the land, and slowly even they recede into Europe and Asia, and Neanderthal Man appears. Then Homo Sapiens makes his final retreat and disappears into the great Rift Valley in Africa, and the world roars to the sound of other beasts and other men. After a pause, Dr When starts his journey back again, this time leaping from place to place, showing where the collections in the British Museum have come from, from the deserts of Assyria to the forests of South America, and the special glut that arrived when Britain ruled the world. Jill leaves the cinema feeling that she can just begin to grasp the scope of this museum.

Sophie and David have reached the display about lions. It is located in two small galleries between the Egyptian and Assyrian collections. The first case lights up as they approach. It contains an oval palette covered with carvings. The glass wall behind it frosts over and a video is projected onto it showing a stretch of savannah, on which lions, ibex and ostriches roam. A hare leaps past in the foreground. Then Sophie notices that all these animals have been carved, in an amazingly lifelike way, on the palette. She learns that lions lived in Egypt and Mesopotamia long before man, and that they were common 45 lifetimes ago when this palette was carved, and survived in the region right up until only 3 lifetimes ago. No one knows what the palette was used for, perhaps for grinding minerals to use as cosmetics, or making magic potions. Even in those early times, a male lion with its splendid mane was regarded as the king of the beasts, and they were associated with the gods. The headset asks if they want to find out more about lions as kings or lions as gods. Sophie is very fond of the Disney film *The Lion King*, and so nods at the first choice.

Sophie's headset leads her to a life-size carving of a recumbent lion, wonderfully relaxed and proud. It is made of polished stone, though it looks so soft she wants to stroke it. She learns that the lion guarded the temple dedicated to the King of Egypt. She looks next at a tiny seal made of agate, which shows two lions rising on their hind legs on either side of a pillar. Two similar, rearing lions guarded the gate to the Royal city of Mycenae, as she can see from the photograph behind. Wild lions would have roamed around its high, stone walls. In the gallery are displays showing how lions have been associated with kings since then, and are included on the British Royal family's coat of arms, but Sophie is not interested in looking at these. She wants to see real lions, and is shown a statue of one that used to grace the railings of the British Museum, she is told, and was modelled on a cat, though it does not look much like a cat to her. She is then led into the next room, but warned that she might find some of the scenes upsetting.

Sophie finds herself in a dark, narrow room lined with carvings on the walls that she can barely make out. She is attracted first to a small video screen in front of a seat. She sits down to watch it. It shows a wild desert landscape where lions roamed. Then a reconstruction of the walls of the Palace of Ashurbanipal, built 40 lifetimes ago, rises before her. The gates are covered with beautiful blue and gold tiles and the camera approaches them. Sophie is then taken inside, through great halls and down corridors, until she is in the very room in which she is now sitting. She looks at the image on the screen and at the room around her. It is exactly the same, except that the walls on the screen are brightly painted to show a sandy landscape under a bright blue sky, with bronzed men in bright red, gold and blue armour, riding in golden chariots or standing in splendid ranks upon the ground. She does not notice the lions at first because their colouring is so similar to that of the sand. Then she sees that they are being killed, shot by arrows flying everywhere through the air, from the soldiers' bows. Blood gushes from their wounds. She cannot bear to look, and turns to stare at the dingy walls around her. Then, slowly, she begins to make out the ghost of the scene she has just been watching on the screen. Intrigued, she goes up to examine the carvings in greater detail. Lions are coming out of the shadows all around her. Their faces are so convincing. One is making a last weary effort to lick its wound. Whoever had carved these lions really loved them, Sophie cannot help thinking, much more than the men who were killing them. And she is even angrier when she sees that the lions did not have a chance. They had been let out of cages into an enclosure so that the king, standing in the centre, could easily kill them.

Sophie learns on her headset that lions at that time were very common, and that if she had gone outside the city walls, she could well have been killed by one. She learns, too, that the king had to be strong, and if he were so strong that he could kill a lion with his bare hands, his people would be safe. The roar of the lions was believed to echo the anger of the God of Thunder, and the flash of the arrows the fury of the God of Lightning. She hears the sound of a storm on her headset, and the whole scene is transformed into a celebration of the power of the gods in the sky and the king on earth, a sort of re-enactment of the battle in the heavens during a thunderstorm; a brutal performance, perhaps, to ensure rain.

But, Sophie cannot help thinking, what about the poor lions? Killing lions was then a sign of people's respect for them, she is told, and they also kept some lions as pets. Her headset leads her to a carving showing one of the king's tame lionesses asleep on a bed of flowers. She looks so content that the king could not have been all that bad, Sophie thinks. She would really love to draw this lioness, and imagine all the colours of the flowers. David offers to go back to the Great Court and hire a drawing set that they had seen when they came in, while Sophie asks the assistant for a stool from the stack that are hanging on the wall behind him. She sits and looks at the carving again, thinking what the world would have been like full of lions – how terrifying and beautiful it would have been. David returns with the drawing board and crayons, and decides to leave Sophie there, in the good care of the assistant, to explore the museum on his own.

As he is passing back through the lion gallery, David notices a sculpture with a woman's head on a lion's body and great eagle's wings. He puts on his headset and learns that this is the famous sphinx, which ate anyone who could not solve the riddle: 'What animal has four feet in the morning, two at midday and three in the evening?' When Oedipus came along and answered 'man', she threw herself off the mountain to her death. His headset asks if he would like to learn more about Greek mythology, or the ages of man. He thinks the latter a bit too close for comfort, and so chooses the former. He is beginning to get the hang of this museum. His headset guides him into the first Greek Gallery and he is initially attracted to an Athenian funeral relief, which depicts a boy, an adult and an old man. After telling him about it, his headset again asks if he would like to see other examples of the ages of man. It is clear he cannot escape this subject, so he decides to go with it. The headset takes him on a fascinating tour through several galleries in the museum, showing him the ways that different cultures have understood and valued the ageing process. He becomes painfully aware how short one lifetime is to learn about life. He passes what he later discovers to be one of several contemplation galleries, in which headsets do not operate and silence reigns. Visitors are encouraged to sit and look at the objects in peace. Short texts explain the value placed on contemplation in different societies. This one, called 'study to be quiet', deals with medieval Christian society. David promises himself to come back to the museum another day to find the Chinese contemplation gallery, which the panel tells him is extensive.

Jake's headset leads him into the King's Library. The interior of the space is huge and rather dark; the walls are lined with books. It feels like he imagines a dusty old museum should. In the distance, Jake can see a stuffed giraffe, its head almost touching the ceiling. Facing him is a strange, dark shining disc. He can just see his face reflected in it. He learns that it was one of the first things ever acquired by the British Museum. It belonged to Dr John Dee, Queen Elizabeth I's astrologer, who had been responsible for calculating the most auspicious day for her coronation. Jake learns that most people, if not everyone, in the past believed that their fate lay in the hands of good and evil spirits who lived, invisibly, all around them. They took great care that they did nothing to offend them. All unexplained phenomena in the natural world – and for many virtually everything was unexplained, even procreation – gave rise to wonder and lively speculation. Anything odd was immediately interpreted as a sign that a spirit was offended. Our powerful imaginations, combined with our instinct to interpret everything in terms of personal gain, peopled the world with poetic ghosts, symbols of our hopes and fears. Jake looks at his pale reflection in the dark surface of the mirror. He learns that it had been made in Mexico and had been brought to Europe by the Spanish Conqueror, Hernando Cortés. The Aztecs believed that the mirror had magic powers, and that anyone looking into it could communicate with spirits. For the first time in his life, Jake glimpses, in his own bleached, shadowy face, a world of mystery and imagination.

Jake's headset suggests that he might like to look at more Aztec material, especially since he has registered an interest in football. His curiosity is aroused and he follows the directions. He soon finds himself entering a gallery arranged like a small tennis court. This was where the Sacred Ball game was played, but when Jake learns that the walls of the court were decorated with real skulls, and that the ball was shaped to look like a real human head, he decides he has had enough gruesome fantasies for one day, and nods twice to get his headset to take him to the display about sex. The gallery he now enters is intimate in feeling, though extensive. There are a lot of people here, but his headset somehow makes him feel less exposed and self-conscious than perhaps he would have done without one. As it is, he hardly gets past the first exhibit. It is a painted scroll showing ten scenes of lovemaking by the Japanese artist Katsukawa Shun'ei, who lived three lifetimes ago. At first he does not realise what he is looking at. Each scene shows a couple entwined together on a couch, wrapped in the folds of richly decorated kimonos. It is only after looking at each for some time that he notices areas of naked flesh revealed in unlikely places between the folds. It takes him even longer to work out which bits of flesh belong to whom, and which part of whose body is exposed. But when he does, suddenly the whole configuration makes sense, and so does the expressions on their faces. He has never been so interested in art before. Up until now Jake has assumed that his own times were the most liberal that have ever been, and that sex was something nobody talked about in the past. He is surprised almost everywhere he looks in this display. He almost laughs out loud when he sees a sculpture of a naked man taking a girl from behind, while she bends over a jar and sucks beer through a straw. His headset tells him that the Ancient Babylonians wrote erotic poetry about the benefits of combining sex with alcohol. He finds the Tantric image of an old priest making love to a young girl really disturbing, however, and he is totally unprepared for the phallic imagery that was so widespread in ancient Rome. He cannot help wondering if the shop sells a reproduction of the set of wind chimes made of little bells hanging from an erect penis, which the Romans hung in their gardens to ward off evil spirits. He finds himself looking at a case of small bronze blades, rather relieved to discover that they are not decorated with sexual imagery, but with ships in full sail, and suns and moons and horses. He learns that they are razors that were used in Bronze Age ceremonies to initiate boys into adulthood, at the time of their first shave. He nods when his headset asks him if he would like to see other initiation ceremonies; he is fascinated to learn how other societies dealt with the transition that he himself is now undergoing, and wonders how he would feel if it was not the private process it has become, but the occasion for a public ritual as it had been in the past.

When Jill comes out into the Great Court, she wonders where to start her visit. The film had made the whole history of the world seem interesting. She wanders around the airy space of the Great Court and is almost tempted to join the queue of people waiting to see the special exhibition *The Poor Always Ye Have With You*, about the history of poverty in the world. She sees it is a joint project with museums in Beijing and Delhi, but she does not want to spend time in line. Then two glass panels catch her eye. They are standing upright on the stone flags, each with an arrow pointing to two adjacent doors. It is the images in the panels that interest her: one shows a hologram of a pair of sandals with wings at their heels, and reads, 'Life was not the same'; the other shows a pair of very ordinary sandals that anyone could wear, and reads, 'Life was the same'. She decides to follow the latter. The first thing she sees in the gallery is the pair of sandals she saw in the hologram. They are tiny and made of white leather and beautifully sewn, and were made for a child in Thebes, who lived 50 lifetimes ago. Nearby are some slices of date cake, made at the same time to a recipe still used today. She is surrounded by everyday objects, either real things such as these, or models of them, made in wood or clay and painted, mostly from ancient Egypt and China, shown next to equivalent things made today, which Jill can pick up and compare to those made and used so long ago. She has never felt so in touch with people in the past.

Behind a semi-circular glass wall, she sees a complete reconstruction of a Roman banquet with its benches, a Chinese feast with its chairs, a Native American potlatch with its blankets and painted boxes and a reconstruction of an equivalent meal to the Last Supper, a simple affair which, to her surprise, was taken sitting on the floor. Jill spends a long time in front of each, amazed at what and how much people ate, and listening to the music and songs that could have accompanied their meals. The familiarity of most things makes the differences that more marked. She is surprised by the delicacy and beauty of some of the tableware, particularly the Roman glass plates and bowls, many of which have been coloured and gilded using techniques that, she learns, have never been surpassed. In a nearby case, necklaces spill out of an open box, beside an array of tiny scent bottles. A mirror lies face down, with a beautifully encrusted back. Magnifying glasses set into the walls of the case let her appreciate the incredible skill of the jewellers of ancient Athens – a gold wreath of oak leaves, acorns and cicadas is as delicately veined and intertwined as if it had been cast from life.

A Roman gravestone catches her attention next, with a scene carved on it showing a little girl sitting on a stool, reading. A dog sits beside her with its paw raised, trying to attract her attention. Jill smiles; her dog does the same whenever she sits down to read. The scene is so natural; it is a moment caught across time. Jill learns that the girl died when she was only ten years old. Next to it is a sculpture of two women sitting on the edge of a bed, gossiping. They are clearly sharing a secret, as if they were living today, not 2,000 years ago. Her headset reminds her that she wanted to see displays about women, and Jill allows herself to be led out of this gallery into one about the history of women. She sees prehistoric carvings which could suggest that the earliest of all known societies were matriarchal. She learns about Greek men's ambivalence towards women, encapsulated in their Pandora myth, beautifully illustrated in a painting on a vase, showing the first woman being sent to earth as 'a punishment to all men who eat bread'. She looks at the sculptures from the Temple of Apollo showing the Greeks battling with the Amazons, and the ash line of destruction in soil deposits that marked where Boudicca burned and pillaged Roman Britain. She studies a painting of women from the other side of the world, showing the sophisticated life of Boudicca's contemporaries at the Emperor's court in China. Again and again she is strongly aware that she is looking at women through men's eyes, but she finds it difficult to categorise these impressions in terms of sexual politics, as she would usually have done.

Jill sits down opposite two life-size figures of women, standing near to each other on a plinth. Both are painted and gilded and extremely elegant, and both look down at her with expressions of deep compassion. One she is familiar with, the Christian Madonna; the other, more buxom and tightly robed, is new to her, a representation of the Buddhist spirit, Tara. She is the consort of the Lord of Compassion, and her widespread popularity is due to the courage she gives him to continue the impossible task of saving all beings from suffering. Though almost certainly made by men, and obviously a projection of men's view of the role of women, their profound beauty annihilates simple explanations. Jill's thoughts are only broken when her headset reminds her it is time to meet the others in the Great Court.

David is studying the simple stone sarcophagus of Nicanos the Alexandrian who, as the inscription makes clear, made the Gates for the Temple at Jerusalem. He is listening to the commentary in Yiddish, when a voice tells him that Sophie wants him to join her in the Lion Gallery. The headset guides him along the corridors and he is soon admiring Sophie's picture of a yellow lion in a bed of pink and white flowers. The assistant there comments how good it is and advises them to show it to the assistant in the Education Gallery. They do, and he pins it up on the board, taking down her name and address, and promising to send it back to her after a month. A group of adults and children are just starting a class with a teacher. They are learning how to communicate with signs and symbols, the basic tools of writing. They are using soft clay tablets, and inventing their own hieroglyphics. Sophie wants to join in at once, but the class is full. When Jill joins them, Sophie presses her into booking a place for her next weekend. On the wall nearby is a display showing the evolution of writing. Jill thinks how much in common these early forms have with computer codes. She would like to join the class herself. Jake comes up, as monosyllabic as ever, but less aggressively so. They each leave the museum with vivid memories of the things they have seen, pondering their meaning, and wanting to return.

Though no country has grounds for complacency (and especially not Britain), illiteracy is far less common than it was during the era when today's great museums were founded. Yet, at the same time, it seems that museums may be losing their natural constituency to computers and video, shopping and formula entertainment. Many fear that we are witnessing a hopeless slide into narrowness and mediocrity, against which museums are one of the last bastions. It is too crude to see intellectual standards disappearing with an older generation, as a tide of crass youngsters take the stage. Changes in society are much more subtle and complex than that, and museums cannot escape them by despising and avoiding them. Tempting as they may appear, the techniques of market research and focus groups, supported by intensive advertising, are unlikely to attract visitors to the fragments of the distant past and the treasures of successive ages that museums hold. The task is more sensitive and creative: to observe, reflect and take account of what is taking place in society, its character, its preoccupations and assumptions, while retaining the belief that the collections can speak to virtually everyone, whatever their prejudices and ignorance may initially be.

The task facing museums is an ambitious and even daunting one: to make the visits they provide as beneficial as possible to as many people as possible. They have the resources to do this. They occupy magnificent buildings, many in enviable locations, with untold riches on display and in store. They have staff with great learning and a love for their subjects. They enjoy wide public support; few politicians would dare propose their eradication, even in times of the greatest hardship or tension. And visitors still come to museums, often in droves. Museums are relatively young, only a quarter of a millennium old. They were invented before the discovery of photography, let alone film, TV and computers, and they now have many competitors. If they do not adapt to meet these challenges, our treasures could soon be locked away in high-security stores, with access to them strictly restricted, and ersatz heritage displays and adventure rides filling the halls and galleries instead.

Museums today are like trees in winter: their collections, like closed buds, all holding tight their secrets. They need to become like trees in summer, their collections flowering in the minds of each visitor. The poetic museum will then not be just a repository for past thoughts and fading memories, but will become a palace of wonder and discovery – a home, once again, for the Muses, those magnificent, spirited and inspiring daughters of Memory.

The God Thoth, quartzite, Ancient Egyptian,
c. 1400 BCE. Thoth, the God of Wisdom, was commonly manifested as a baboon.
British Museum

Further Reading – Malraux and Beyond

The Poetic Museum sprang directly from the need that I have perceived during my career to formulate a new, practical philosophy for museums, which eventually took the form of this book. It was informed by countless discussions with colleagues and many years' experience of working in museums, against a background of much professional participation in journals, conferences and books. Here, as a guide to this sea of thought, I can indicate just a few of the books that have helped me chart my course.

There is a rising tide of books that give practical guidance to museum staff on how to protect collections against theft, decay and, nowadays, legal challenges, how to write labels and run educational programmes, how to manage staff and, increasingly, how to raise money. The *Manual of Curatorship* (edited by John M.A. Thompson, Butterworths, London, 1984) and *The Museum; a Reference Guide* (edited by Michael Steven Shapiro with Louis W. Kemp, Greenwood Publishing Group, Westport, CT, USA, 1990), a compendium of information about museums, including histories, are both hefty and worthy tomes. There are Museums Associations in most countries of Northern Europe (not in Spain, Italy or Greece) and in Canada, Australia and the USA, all of which publish journals and arrange conferences. The International Council of Museums (ICOM), based in Paris, attempts, fairly successfully, to do this on an international basis. Most of the extensive literature that these organisations produce is purely for professional interest, and that goes for the majority of books about museology. Standard works of this kind, which have transformed the public's experience of museums worldwide, such as *The Museum Environment* (Garry Thomson, Butterworths, London, 1978) and *The Design of Educational Exhibits* (Roger S. Miles and contributors, Unwin Hyman, London, 1982/8), would lose the general reader on the second page. Almost all of this literature is based on the supposition that museums are fine as they are, although it does attempt to raise standards in whatever aspect of the profession it deals with, whether it be conservation, security, financial control or customer care.

To an outsider reading about museums for the first time, it might seem as though they comprise a conglomerate of professions, rather than a unified one seeking a common goal, so much so that the death of the overseeing curator is increasingly being predicted in the columns of the professional journals, including the *Art Newspaper*, which is the only periodical with a wider readership that deals regularly with museum matters internationally (though mostly in the field of fine and decorative art. There are, of course, countless books about what museums contain, usually published as guides, and increasingly available on the web, but these often tell one little, if anything, about the reason why the collections exist or how they are being developed unless, of course, this involves new buildings, which are usually well marketed. The literature on modern museum building is immense, usually based on individual projects. Victoria Newhouse gives an overview in *Towards A New Museum* (Monacelli, Italy, 1998), and *Museums for a New Millennium* (edited by Vittorio Magnago Lampugnani and Angeli Sachs, Prestel Verlag, New York and Art Centre Basel, 1999) provides detailed case studies, but both deal almost exclusively with art museums. In this literature, one reads more about architecture than museums.

One of the best ways to understand the intentions of museums is to read the literature they produce themselves. Many make public statements in their annual reports, usually in the form of a Director's address, and most of these are now available on individual websites. ICOM runs a virtual library to museum pages: http:/www.icom.org/vlmp. But all this literature is essentially promotional. A better way for an outsider to get a feeling for a museum from the inside is to read the personal accounts of those who have worked in them (usually those who have run them). There are many of these, through history, and I give three recent examples to illustrate the genre. Thomas Hoving, in *Making the Mummies Dance* (Simon and Schuster, New York, 1993) gives a vivid picture of life inside the Metropolitan Museum of Art, from the larger-than-life perspective of a flamboyant Director. David M. Wilson, in *The British Museum, Purposes and Politics* (British Museum Publications, London, 1989), provides a more sober but nevertheless shotgun ride through the labyrinthine practices of the British Museum when he was Director, which is much more readable than its title implies. More profoundly revealing is Martin Harwit's measured account of the tale of the Smithsonian Air And Space Museum's display of the plane that dropped the first atom bomb, in *An Exhibit Denied: Lobbying the History of the Enola Gay* (Copernicus Books, SpringerVerlag, New York, 1996). It reveals a great museum in a dither about its political position, ending up with it effectively withdrawing from the debate, and with Martin Harwit losing his job.

There is not, as yet, a good summary of the history of museums, which gives the general reader an introduction to the intellectual, cultural, social and political contexts that have governed their making and influenced their development up until today. It would be a daunting undertaking, because so much of this history is compartmentalised. Miels von Holst's *Creators, Collectors and Connoisseurs, the Anatomy of Public Taste from Antiquity to the Present*

Day (Thames and Hudson, London, 1967) reveals the implications of the subject, and he only deals with art. Fascinating stories are beginning to emerge, such as Stephen T. Asma's *Stuffed Animals and Pickled Heads: the Culture and Evolution of Natural History Museums* (Oxford University Press, 2001) and Patricia West's *Domesticating History: the Political Origins of America's House Museums* (Smithsonian Institution Press, Washington DC, 1999). Some of the most vivid histories are to be found in books about specific museums; there are thousands of these, usually published by the museums themselves and advertised on their websites. *Inventing the Louvre: Art, Politics and the Origin of the Modern Museum in Eighteenth-Century Paris* by Andrew McClellan (Cambridge University Press, 1994) is a key work, in that it gives a broad account of museum development at a crucial stage in its history; and Geraldine Norman's *The Hermitage – a Biography of a Great Museum* (Pimlico, London, 1999) reveals the large part that personality and chance play in the formation of such great institutions (it is especially good on how the Hermitage survived the Revolution – with the help of the attendants).

Increasingly, writers are beginning to explore the political context of contemporary museum development, for example, in *Creating the Musée d'Orsay: the Politics of Culture in France* by Andrea Kupfer Schneider (Pennsylvania State University Press, 1998), and *Beyond The Prado: Museums and Identity in Democratic Spain* by Selma Holo (Smithsonian Institution Press, 1999), which puts, among other developments, the Guggenheim Museum in Bilbao into its political context.

Counter-balancing all this information about how museums have been and can be run, and what they contain, is an equally large and growing mountain of literature about the theory of cultural provision. These range right the way across the political spectrum, but though they often contain references to museums, few deal with these specifically. Though they are subsidised as heavily as theatres, concert halls and contemporary exhibition spaces (though by no means so extensively as broadcasting), museums have so far seemed almost invisible as institutions capable of making a social and political impact. Heritage organisations working in the fields of both the natural and man-made environment have come under much closer scrutiny than museums themselves. *The Heritage Industry: Britain in a Climate of Decline* by Robert Hewison (Methuen, London, 1987), for example, was an early attack on historic theme parks that left museums virtually unscathed. Questioning attitudes are now emerging about museums and their collections, but usually within specific disciplines, rather than across the profession as a whole. Ethnographic collections, for long a backwater, have become increasingly interesting to scholars researching the impact of colonisation and independence

171

on cultural history and politics. *Reinventing Africa: Museums, Material Culture and Popular Imagination* by Annie E. Coombs (Yale University Press, New Haven and London, 1994) charts the way that museum collections reflected and influenced public perception of Africa in the 19th and early 20th centuries; and Moira McLoughlin deals with contemporary issues in *Museums and the Interpretation of Native Canadians: Negotiating the Borders of Culture* (Garland Publishing, 1999). The field of contemporary art is veined with controversy, but among all the literature this has generated, remarkably little attention has been paid to the role of museums and their reasons for giving the oxygen of publicity to some controversies and not to others. Sir Nicholas Serota, in his Walter Neurath Memorial Lecture *Experience or Interpretation: The Dilemma of Museums of Modern Art* (Thames and Hudson, London, 2000), chose to talk about how museums present modern art and how they need to work closer with artists, and not to address the more fundamental dilemma of what they collect and why. Again and again the power base of the museum sails past unchallenged. Mary Anne Staniszewski intrepidly entered this terrain in *The Power of Display: A History of Exhibition Installation at the Museum of Modern Art* (MIT Press, 1998), and Steven C. Dubin has opened the debate wider by investigating public disputes based around museums in *Displays of Power: Controversy in the American Museum from Enola Gay to Sensation* (New York University Press, 2000).

The status of museum collections themselves is increasingly coming under much closer scrutiny. Several museums now openly display and publish information about their fakes, and David Phillips has explored this whole issue in *Exhibiting Authenticity* (Manchester University Press, 1997). Many writers, mostly from outside the museum profession, have mused upon the meaning of things they have seen in museums. Stephen E. Weil is one of the few to have done so from a background of working within museums, and I am most closely in sympathy with what he has written in his books *Rethinking Museums and Other Meditations* and *A Cabinet of Curiosities: Inquiries into Museums and their Prospects* (1990 and 1995, both Smithsonian Institution Press).

I began my career in museums feeling that I was trying to row against the tide, but I now feel part of a groundswell of change. Many books indicate this new direction. Jeshajahu Weinberg revealed some of his philosophy in his account, with Rina Elieli, of the making of *The Holocaust Museum in Washington* (Rizzoli International Publications, New York, 1995). Peter Greenaway's *Flying Out of this World (The Parti-Pris Series)* (University of Chicago Press, 1994) gives a taste of what his experimental exhibition at the Louvre was like. If you cannot get to see the Museum of Jurassic Technology in Los Angeles, Lawrence Weschler's account of it in *Mr Wilson's Cabinet of*

Wonder (Vintage Books, New York, 1999) is nearly as good as being there. Many of the museums mentioned in this book have publications dedicated to them, though few are served so evocatively as this.

This book was written with the museum visitor in mind. One of the few books about museums ever to catch the attention of a wider public was *Le Musée Imaginaire* by André Malraux (Editions Gallimard, Paris, 1965), translated into English as *Museum Without Walls* by Stuart Gilbert and Francis Price (Secker & Warburg, London, 1967), but perhaps that is because it is not really about museums at all. It is a muse upon the changing nature of art today. It argues that, for the first time in our history, we can now appreciate, by means of colour reproductions, the whole panoply of humanity's artistic production, from all ages and all cultures. That is the Museum Without Walls. By comparison, even the largest museums can only give us a fragmentary glimpse of this achievement, and when they do so, Malraux argues, they inevitably show it stripped of its original function (in many cases its sanctity) and placed, instead, within an intellectual context. 'Art', he wrote, 'doesn't belong to knowledge, but to life'. Images in books are therefore better because they are unframed – they allow us to imagine what the work of art might have meant to its original user, while responding to what it means to us today. In the process, Malraux believed, we will, as we survey the whole artistic achievement of humanity, discover a new meaning in art, 'the song of metamorphosis – and no one before us has heard it – the song in which aesthetics, dreams, and even religions are no more than librettos to an inexhaustible music'. This discovery would, Malraux suggested, lead people back to look at real things in museums, and these institutions would in time develop new forms as yet unknown, to express this new view of art. Boldly, but humbly, I claim Malraux as my mentor. I have attempted in this book to articulate a new form for museums, not just for their art collections, but for everything they contain. The 'song of metamorphosis', when art and religion come together with our aspirations, will, I believe, be heard in the poetic museum.

List of Museums

List of Museums mentioned in the text, giving address, telephone number and website when available

Australia

Australian Museum; 6-8 College Street, Sydney NSW 2000; (+ 61 2) 93206000; www.amonline.net.au

National Gallery of Victoria; Victorian Art Centre, 180 Saint Kilda Road, Melbourne 3004; (+ 61 3) 92080220

National Museum of Australia, POB 1901 Canberra ACT 2601; (+ 61 2) 62561111

Austria

Albertina, Albertina Platz 1, 1010 Vienna; (+ 43 1) 534 83 0; www.albertina.at

Kunsthistorisches Museum, Maria-Theresian-Platz, 1010 Vienna (+ 43 1) 525 24 0; www.khm.at

Natural History Museum, Maria-Theresian-Platz, 1010 Vienna; (+ 43 1) 52177; www.nhm-wien.ac.at

Canada

Canadian Museum of Civilization, 100 Laurier Street (PO Box 3100), Station B, Hull, Quebec J8X 4HZ; (+ 819) 776 7000; www.civilization.ca/cmc/cmce.asp

Denmark

Johannes Larsen Museum, Møllebakken, 5300 Kerteminde; (+ 45) 65323727; www.kert-mus.dk/jhl/dk/main.html

Louisiana Museum of Modern Art, GL Strandvej 13, 3050 Humlebæk; (+ 45) 49190719; www.louisiana.dk

National Museum of Denmark (Nationalmuseet), Prinsens Palais, Frederiksholms Kanal 12, 1220 Copenhagen K; (+ 45) 33134411

Nordjyllands Art Museum, Kong Christians Allé 50, 9000 Aalborg; (+45) 98138088

Ny Carlsberg Glyptotek, Dantes Pl 7, 1556 Copenhagen V; (+ 45) 33418141

Statens Museum for Kunst, Sølvgade 48-50, 1307 Copenhagen K; (+ 45) 33748494; www.kulturnet.dk/homes/smk

Women's Museum (Kvindemuseet i Danmark) Domkirkeplads 5, 8000 Aarhus C; (+ 45) 86136144

Egypt

Museum of Egyptian Antiquities, Midan El Tahrir, Kasr El Nil, Sharia Selim Hassan, 11556 Cairo; (+ 20 2) 775133

France

Louvre, 34-36 quai du Louvre, 75058 Paris Cedex 01; (+ 33 1) 40 20 50 50; www.louvre.fr

Pompidou Centre, rue Beaubourg, 75004 Paris; (+ 33 1) 44 78 12 33; www.cnac-gp.fr

Germany

Glyptothek, Königsplatz 1-3, D-80333 Munich; (+ 49 89) 598359

Jewish Museum, Lindenstr. 9–14, D-10969 Berlin; (+ 49 30) 308785681; www.jmberlin.de

Neanderthal Museum, Talstr. 300, D-40822 Mettmann; (+ 49 2104) 979797; www.neanderthal.de

Israel

Israel Museum, POB 71117 Jerusalem 91710; (+ 972) 2 670 8811; www.imj.org.il

Museum of the History of Jerusalem, The Tower of David, David Street, Jerusalem; (+ 972) 2 626 5333

Museum of the Jewish Diaspora, Klausner Street, Tel Aviv-Jaffa, 69011; (+ 972) 3 646 2020; www.bh.org.il

Italy

Brancacci Chapel in Santa Maria del
Carmine, Florence;
giubileo.comune.fi.it/musei/brancacci

Castelvecchio Museum, Corso Castelvecchio 2, 37121 Verona;
(+ 39 045) 594734

Egyptian Museum, Via Accademia delle
Scienze 6, 10123 Turin; (+ 39 011)
5617776

Museum of the History of Science, Piazza
dei Giudici 1, 50122 Florence;
(+ 39 055) 293493;
imss@galileo.imss.firenze.it

Museum of Maquettes, Via S. Agostino 1,
Pietrasanta; (0584) 791122

National Museum of the Bargello, Via del
Proconsolo 4, Florence

South Tyrol Museum of Archaeology
(Museo Archeologico dell'Alto Adige),
Via Museo 43, Bolzano;
(+ 39 0476) 982098;
museo@iceman.it; www.iceman.it

Uffizi, Piazzale degli Uffizi,
50122 Florence; (+ 39 055) 2388651

Vatican Museums, Viale Vaticano 00120,
Citta del Vaticano; (+ 39 06) 69883333

Japan

Kumamoto Castle, 1-1 Honmaru,
Kumamoto

The Netherlands

Groninger Museum, Museumeiland 1,
9711 ME Groningen; (+ 31 50) 3666555

Rijksmuseum, Stadhouderskade 42,
1071 ZD Amsterdam; (+ 31 20)
6732121;
www.rijksmuseum.nl

New Zealand

Te Papa Tangarewa Museum of New
Zealand, PO Box 467, Wellington;
64 4 381 7000

Norway

Viking Ships Museum (Vikingskipene),
Huk Aveny 35, Bygdøy, 0287 Oslo 2;
(+ 47) 22416300

Munch Museum, Toyengaten 53, P.b. 2812
Toyen, N-0608 Oslo; (+ 47) 23241400;
www.museumsnett.no/munchmuseet

Russia

State Museum of Political History of
Russia, ul Kuibysheva 4,
197046 St Petersburg;
(+ 7 812) 2337266

Singapore

Asian Civilizations Museum, 93 Armenian
Street, Singapore, 179941; (+ 65) 332
3284; www.museum.org.sg/ACM

Tang Dynasty City, Yuan Ching Road,
Singapore; (+ 65) 261 1116

Spain

Guggenheim Museum, Av. Abandoibarra 2,
48001 Bilbao; (+ 34 94) 4359000

Prado, Paseo del Prado, 28014 Madrid;
(+ 34 91) 3302800

Sweden

Vasa Museum, Statens Sjöhistoriska
Museer, Galärvarvet, Djurgården,
102 52 Stockholm; (+ 46 8) 519 548 00;
www.vasamuseet.se

Switzerland

Ethnographic Museum, Augustinergasse 2,
CH-4051 Basel; (+ 41) 61 266 5500

Natural History Museum, Augustinergasse
2, CH-4001 Basel, Switzerland;
(+ 41 61) 266 5500; www.nmb.bs.ch

Taiwan

National Palace Museum, Wai-shuang-hsi,
Shih-lin, Taipei; (+ 886 2) 28812021;
www.npm.gov.tw

UK

England

Ashmolean Museum, Beaumont Street,
Oxford OX1 2PH; (+ 44 1865) 278000;
www.ashmol.ox.ac.uk

British Library, 96 Euston Road, London
NW1 2DB; (+ 44 207) 412 7000;
www.bl.uk

British Museum, Great Russell Street,
London WC1B 3DG; (+ 44 207) 636
1555; www.british-museum.ac.uk

Cartwright Hall, Lister Park,
Bradford BD9 4NS; (+ 44 1274) 751212

1853 Gallery, Salts Mill, Victoria Road,
Saltaire, Shipley BD18 3LB; (+ 44 1274)
531163; www.saltsmill.org.uk

Gallery of English Costume, Platt Hall,
Rusholme, Manchester M14 5LL;
(+ 44 161) 224 5217

Gilbert Collection, Somerset House,
Victoria Embankment, London;
(+ 44 207) 845 4000;
www.somerset-house.org.uk

Imperial War Museum, Lambeth Road,
London SE1 6HZ; (+ 44 207) 416 5000;
www.iwm.org.uk

Kelham Island Industrial Museum, Alma
Street, off Corporation Street, Sheffield;
(+ 44 114) 272 2106; www.shu.ac.uk

Kettle's Yard, Cambridge, Castle Street,
Cambridge CB3 0AQ; (+ 44 1223)
352124; kettles-yard-gen@lists.cam.ac.uk

Manchester City Art Gallery, Mosley Street,
Manchester M2 3JL; (+ 44 161) 236
5244; www.u-net.com/set/mcag/
cag.html

Manchester Museum, University of
Manchester, Oxford Road, Manchester
M13 9PL;
(+ 44 161) 275 2634

Museum of Science and Industry in
Manchester, Liverpool Road, Manchester
M3 4FP; (+ 44 161) 832 2244

National Gallery, Trafalgar Square, London
WC2N 5DN;
(+ 44 207) 747 2885;
www.nationalgallery.org.uk

National Maritime Museum,
Romney Road, London SE10 9NF;
(+ 44 208) 858 4422

Natural History Museum, Cromwell Road,
London SW7 5BD; (+ 44 207) 938 9123;
www.nhm.ac.uk

Nottingham Castle Museum and Art Gallery, Castle, off Friar Lane, Nottingham
NG1 6EL; (+ 44 115) 915 3700

Pitt Rivers Museum, South Parks Road,
Oxford OX1 3PW; (+ 44 1865) 272950

Pump House: People's History Museum
(National Museum of Labour History),
Left Bank Street, Manchester M3 3ER;
(+ 44 161) 839 6061

Ruskin Gallery, Collection of the Guild
of St George, 101 Norfolk Street,
Sheffield S1 2JE; (+ 44 114) 273 5299

Science Museum, Exhibition Road,
London SW7 2DD; (+ 44 207) 938
8000; www.nmsi.ac.uk

Tate Britain, Millbank. London SW1P
4RG; (+ 44 207) 887 8000;
www.tate.org.uk/britain

Tate Modern, Bankside, London SE1 9TG;
(+ 44 207) 887 8000;
www.tate.org.uk/modern

Temple Newsam House, Leeds LS15 0AE;
(+ 44 113) 264 7321

Victoria & Albert Museum, Cromwell
Road, London SW7 2RL; (+ 44 207)
942 2000;
www.vam.co.uk

Walker Art Gallery, William Brown Street,
Liverpool L3 8EL; (+ 44 151) 478 4199

Whitworth Art Gallery, Oxford Road,
Manchester M15 6ER;
(+ 44 161) 275 7450;
www.man.ac.uk/wag

Scotland

Burrell Collection, Pollok Country Park,
2060 Pollokshaws Road,
Glasgow G43 1AT;
(+ 44 141) 649 7151

Gallery of Modern Art, Queen Street,
Glasgow G1 1DT; (+ 44 141) 229 1996;
www.goma.gov.uk

Heatherbank Museum of Social Work,
City Campus, Cowcaddens Road, Glasgow G4 0BA; (+ 44 141) 331 3921;
www.lib.gcal.ac.uk/heatherbank

Kelvingrove Museum and Art Gallery,
Glasgow G3 8AG; (+ 44 141) 287 2699

Museum of Scotland, Chambers Street,
Edinburgh, EH1 1JF; (+ 44 131) 247
4422; www.nms.ac.uk/mos

Museum of Transport, Kelvin Hall,
1 Bunhouse Road, Glasgow G3 8DP;
(+ 44 141) 287 2720

National Gallery of Scotland, The Mound,
Edinburgh E2; (+ 44 131) 220 0917;
www.natgalscot.ac.uk

Open Museum, Martyr's School,
Parson Street, Glasgow G4 0PX;
(+ 44 141) 552 2356

Our Dynamic Earth, Holyrood Road,
Edinburgh EH8 8AS; (+ 44 131) 550
7800; www.dynamicearth.co.uk

People's Palace Museum, Glasgow Green,
Glasgow G40 1AT; (+ 44 141) 544 0223

Wales

Glynn Vivian Art Gallery, Alexandra Road,
Swansea SA1 5DZ; (+ 44 1792) 655006

National Museum and Gallery of Wales,
Cathays Park, Cardiff CF1 3NP;
(+ 44 1222) 397951

United States of America

The Art Institute of Chicago, 111 S Michi-
gan Avenue, Chicago, IL 60603-6110;
(+ 1 312) 443 3600

The Children's Museum, Museum Wharf,
300 Congress Street,
Boston, MA 02210-1034;
(+ 1 617) 426 6500

EMP (Experience Music Project),
325 5th Avenue N., Seattle, WA 98019;
(+1 206) 367 5483;
www.emplive.com

The Exploratorium, 3601 Lyon Street, San
Francisco, CA 94123; (+ 1 415) 563
7337; www.exploratorium.edu

Field Museum of Natural History,
Roosevelt Road at Lake Shore Drive,
Chicago, IL 60605; (+ 1 312) 922 9410

The Frick Collection, 1 East 70th Street,
New York, NY 10021; (+ 1 212) 288
0700

J Paul Getty Museum, 17985 Pacific Coast
Highway, Malibu, CA 90265-5799;
(+ 1 310) 458 2003;
www.getty.edu/museum

Solomon R Guggenheim Museum, 1071
Fifth Avenue at 88th Street, New York,
NY10128; (+ 1 212) 423 3500

Los Angeles County Museum of Art,
5905 Wilshire Boulevard, Los Angeles,
CA 90036; (+ 1 213) 857 6000;
www.lacma.org

Metropolitan Museum of Art, 5th Avenue at
82nd Street, New York, NY 10028-0198;
(+ 1 212) 879 5500

Minnesota History Centre, 345 Kellogg
Boulevard W, St Paul, MN 55102-1906

Museum of Jurassic Technology,
9341 Venice Boulevard, Culver City,
Los Angeles, CA 90232;
(+ 1 310) 836 6131; www.mjt.org

Museum of Modern Art, 11 W 53rd Street,
New York, NY 10019;
(+ 1 212) 708 9480

Museum of Tolerance, Simon Wiesenthal
Plaza, 9786 West Pico Boulevard,
Los Angeles, CA 90035;
(+ 1 310) 553 8403;
www.wiesenthal.com/mot

New-York Historical Society, 2 West 77th
Street, New York, NY 10024;
(+ 1 212) 873 3400; www.nyhistory.org

Smithsonian Institution, 1000 Jefferson
Drive SW, Washington DC;
(+ 1 202) 357 2700; www.si.edu

United States Holocaust Memorial
Museum, 100 Raoul Wallenberg
Place SW, Washington, DC 20024;
(+ 1 202) 488 0400;
www.ushmm.org

Index of Names

Page references in italics refer to illustrations; those in bold refer to text in boxes.

Index compiled by Christine Shuttleworth